T · H · E
Four-Course
400-Calorie Meal
C · O · O · K · B · O · O · K

NANCY S. HUGHES

CB
CONTEMPORARY
BOOKS
CHICAGO

Library of Congress Cataloging-in-Publication Data

Hughes, Nancy S.
    The four-course, 400-calorie meal cookbook : quick and easy
recipes for delicious low-calorie, low-fat dinners / Nancy S.
Hughes.
        p.   cm.
    Includes index.
    ISBN 0-8092-4058-0 (pbk.) :
    1. Low-calorie diet—Recipes.   2. Low-fat diet—Recipes.
I. Title.
RM222.2.H85   1991
641.5'635—dc20   90-25491
                                                  CIP

Published by Contemporary Books, Inc.
Two Prudential Plaza, Chicago, Illinois 60601-6790
Manufactured in the United States of America
International Standard Book Number: 0-8092-4058-0

This book is lovingly dedicated to my family:

Will, my fourteen-year-old son, for his sense of humor when experiments failed.

Annie, my eleven-year-old daughter, for her diplomatic yet honest comments.

Taft, my six-year-old son, for his ever-faithful assistance in the kitchen.

And Greg, my husband, for his endurance, patience, sometimes unwanted advice, and, above all, his capability to pay the enormous grocery bill.

❧ CONTENTS ❧

✦ PREFACE ✦

I love the warmth felt when the family is gathered around the dinner table.

I love entertaining on the patio, with lively conversations and the smell of barbecue in the air.

I love family get-togethers, with tables filled with good foods.

I love picnicking under a shady tree in the quiet of the woods.

I love sharing a lunch with my little ones—a lunch we've made together.

I love quiet conversations with my husband over a candlelit dinner.

I love life, and I love food and the special atmospheres one can create around it. Why should these be sacrificed when you are counting calories? Life and its precious moments are too valuable to set aside. It doesn't have to be that way anymore.

Enjoy!

❊ ACKNOWLEDGMENTS ❊

I want to thank my parents for their high aspirations and for their love of good food.

Thanks also go to:

Kathy Strawn, for reading my mind and actually making sense of it; Eunice Swift, for critiquing my recipes and giving me valuable advice; my friends and relatives, who had to live with me through it all—good days and bad—and remained my friends and relatives; my butchers, for their time and expertise; the many dietitians I consulted, for their generous advice and assistance in calculating calorie contents; and, finally, my precious husband and children, who endured the writing, testings, and calculating and still love me.

1
❊ INTRODUCTION ❊

This book contains recipes for salads, entrees, vegetables, and desserts—all low in calories, all low in fat. These dishes can be combined to produce hundreds of delicious four-course meals that *never exceed 400 calories*. All of the calorie counting has been done for you, and the meal-planning chart lets you select, at a glance, the dishes you might wish to combine for any particular meal.

Why did I write this book? Because by the sixth day of subsisting on a popular liquid diet I was ready to devour my own children! I also realized how ridiculous our family dinner hour had become. I found myself cooking and serving a delicious dinner (and cleaning up afterward, I might add) to my husband and three children while I had my "dinner in a glass" on the porch. Grumbling and stewing, with glass in hand, I recalled the sage words of the representative of this insane diet method. "If you think about it," she commented, "how much food could you eat for so few calories?" The expected answer: "Not much!"

I had tried numerous diet plans and found them all very isolating—whether they involved drinking alone on the porch or preparing my own separate meal. That's when my search began for tasty, light meals that my family and I, as a dieter, could enjoy together. Wouldn't their health as well as mine benefit from less fat? I wanted three- and four-course meals at my fingertips that were consistently low in calories. And since I had to appeal to children whose ages range from six to fourteen, plus a husband who possesses a love of good food, I was forced to keep the taste factor high (not an easy assignment!). With a little planning and a little research, though, I discovered that our family *could* maintain a sensible eating plan and become a "one-meal family" again!

In the process of research I found that many popular "light" recipes can be deceiving. "Light" does not always mean low in calories. When I combined recipes from well-known "light" cookbooks for a salad, vegetable, entree, and dessert, the calorie count would vary from 400 to 900 calories. That 500-calorie difference could actually be another entire meal!

After six years of trial and error experimentation and research, I've developed and refined more than 200 recipes that are consistently low in calories. All salads, vegetables, and desserts total only 50 calories each; all main dishes have no more than 250 calories. A complete meal, then, will always total 400 delicious calories or less, and all are low in fat. They are based on easily obtainable, natural ingredients (many are low in sodium and cholesterol). As for preparation, the recipes are easy to follow, and many can be prepared in 15 minutes or less! (You'll also find them to be a great mealtime resource if you have just completed a diet and are trying to keep off those pounds.)

Suggested accompaniments and helpful hints appear below main dish recipes, along with the calculated fat grams per serving to help you keep track of your fat intake. These additions, along with the meal-planning chart, make meal preparation easy. Don't overlook the "Plain and Simple" sections of each recipe chapter; they can be a lifesaver. When there's just enough time for preparation, and planning is out of the question, these lists will tell you, for example, how many ounces of broiled chicken you may have for 250 calories or how many green beans you are allowed for 50 calories.

Evenings, I have found, can be especially discouraging for the calorie-conscious. During the day calorie intake is easier to control, but when the sun goes down and the family members reunite, fatigue chases away those good intentions begun at breakfast. This cookbook was written, in part, to eliminate the need for you to prepare two evening meals—one for the dieter(s) and one for the other household members. It was also written to help simplify busy lives—to let you stop the calorie counting at dinnertime and start enjoying delicious meals *with* your family and friends again!

2
AT-A-GLANCE
❧ MEAL-PLANNING CHART ❧

Salads—Gelatin

Bountifully Layered Salad (11)
A Family Reunion Salad (12)
Orange-Kiwi Ginger (10)

Spicy Peaches (12)
Tangy Cranberry Fiesta Salad (9)

Salads—Fruit

Caribbean Fruit Salad (13)
Fruited Melon Wedges (14)
Gingered Fruit Kabobs (15)

Hot Curried Fruit (14)
Raspberry-Glazed Peaches (13)
Waldorf Salad (15)

Salads—Vegetable

Carrot and Bell Pepper Salad (20)
Corn Medley (20)
Creamy Cucumbers (17)
Europe's Pride (16)
A Friend's Green Chili Salad (21)
From a Corner of Chinatown (18)
Garden and Pasta Salad (22)

Lemon-Limed Tomatoes (19)
Mandarin Salad with Almonds (19)
Marinated Mushrooms with Blue
    Cheese (16)
Old-Fashioned Coleslaw (17)
The Stacked Salad (18)
Summer's Cucumbers (21)

Salad Dressings

Chinatown Soy (24)
Creamy Avocado Dressing (25)
Creamy Dijon (29)
Creamy Garlic with Parmesan (28)
Italian's Italian (26)
Simply Blue (24)

Smooth and Creamy Blue (28)
Sweet Basil Vinaigrette (27)
Sweet Honey Mustard Dressing (23)
Thousand Island Dressing (29)
Zesty Lemon Vinaigrette (26)

Main Courses—Poultry

Apricot "Ham" Steak (63)
Barbecued Chicken Breasts (39)
Broiled Chicken Breasts with Herbed Vegetable Rice (38)
Broiled Spicy Mustard Chicken (40)
Cheesy Corn and "Ham" Chowder (44)
Chicken à l'Orange (32)
Chicken and Broccoli Oriental (43)
Chicken and Wild Rice Casserole (48)
Chicken Burgundy (41)
Chicken Dijon (42)
Chicken in a Pot (52)
Chicken Monterey (59)
Chicken Sizzler (36)
Chicken Supreme (64)
Chicken with Blue Cheese (35)
"Ham" and Potato Casserole in Cheese Sauce (45)
Hearty Country Chicken Soup (51)
Individual Potato Puffs (60)
Jalapeño, Bean, and "Ham" Soup with Cheese (62)
Lemon Chicken with Almonds (46)
Lemon Curry Chicken with Broccoli and Cheese (57)
Mandarin Chicken Salad (50)
My Annie's Favorite (34)
Old Bay Chicken with Broccoli-Rice Casserole (37)
Peppered Chicken Teriyaki (33)
Roasted Chicken Breasts (53)
Scalloped "Ham" and Potato Casserole (61)
Sicilian Chicken Soup (47)
Simko's Cacciatore (55)
Skewered Chicken and Beef Oriental (65)
Smothered Chicken (54)
Southern Oven-Fried Chicken (56)
Special-Occasion Chicken (58)
Thai-Style Hot Curried Chicken (49)

Main Courses—Seafood

Baked Flounder with Creamy Tarragon Sauce (78)
Baked Flounder with New Potatoes in Lemon Butter (83)
Baked Snapper with Herbed Butter (82)
The Bay's Best Seafood Gumbo (66)
Brown-Buttered Fish with Toasted Almonds (80)
Crab Casserole with Cheese (68)
Crab Geneva (67)
Crab Quiche with Wine (65)
Curried Shrimp Deluxe (72)
Deviled Crab and Shrimp Supreme (69)
Fish Cakes Drizzled with Butter (81)
Flounder and Bacon Kabobs with Creamy Baked Potatoes (79)
Flounder Meunière (84)
Flounder Parmesan (85)
Flounder with Green Bell Peppers and Border Rice (77)
Hot Buttered Shrimp (70)
Linguine with Clam Sauce (86)
Oriental Shrimp Balls with Sauces (76)
A Sailor's Barbecue (74)
Shrimp and Mushrooms Elégante (75)
Shrimp Creole (73)
Shrimp Salad with Fresh Lemon (71)

Main Courses—Beef

All-American Beef Stew (92)
Beef and Green Chili Casserole (108)
Beef Burgundy (89)
Beef Kabobs (95)
Beef Roasted with Garlic and Wine (87)
Beef Stroganoff with Dill (105)
Broiled Steak in Hot Honey Mustard (94)
Creamy Beef Casserole with Scallions (101)
Eunice's Swedish Meatballs (107)
A Family Casserole (104)
Green Pepper Steak (88)
Hot and Spicy Meatball Soup (99)
Hungarian Goulash (90)

A Lebanese Favorite (106)
Marinated Steak with Horseradish
    Sauce (93)
Meatballs and Gravy (100)
Mexico's Finest Soufflé (103)
Moussaka (103)
Pan-Fried Steak with Red Wine Sauce (109)
Saturday's Meat Loaf (98)
Simplicity (91)
Skillet Rio Grande (102)
Steak with Zesty Whipped "Butter" (96)
Stuffed Cheeseburgers (97)

Main Courses—Pork

Chinatown Cabbage Rolls (113)
Peppered Pork Tenderloin (114)
Pork and Peppers with Pineapple Rice (118)
Simply Pork Chops (112)
Skewered Pork and Orange Curry (115)

Skewered Pork with Honey Mustard
    Glaze (117)
Skillet Pork (111)
Szechwan Pork and Vegetables (116)

Main Courses—Meatless

Asparagus and Vegetable Casserole (128)
Cheesy Onion Casserole (134)
Cream Cheese and Noodles with
    Scallions (120)
Creamy Cheese Quiche (124)
The Decadent Crustless Quiche (123)
Individual Refried Bean Casseroles (125)
Linguine and Vegetables (119)
Oriental Stuffed Pitas (126)
The Overloaded Pizza (122)

Pie Parmesan (130)
Rainy Day Broccoli Soup with Jalapeño
    Corn Muffins (131)
Sautéed Cabbage with Noodles (129)
Spinach-and Cheese-Stuffed
    Manicotti (133)
Tortilla Soup with Cilantro (132)
Triple Cheese Lasagna (121)
Zucchini and Cheese Casserole (127)

Vegetables

Desserts

3
❧ YOUR SHOPPING LIST ❧

The following packaged items are used in many of the recipes in this book. Be sure to select these products according to the calorie contents listed below.

Bouillon Granules (Beef or Chicken, Prepared): 16 calories per ½ cup (I use Campbell's)

Bread, Diet (Extra-Thin): 35 calories per slice (I use Pepperidge Farm's Light 'n Natural)

Broth, Undiluted: *Beef*—40 calories per ½ cup (I use Campbell's)
  Chicken—35 calories per ½ cup (I use Campbell's)

Catsup, Lite: 8 calories per tablespoon (I use Heinz Lite)

Cheese: *cheddar, reduced-fat*—80 calories per ounce (I use Kraft Light Naturals)
  Monterey Jack, reduced fat—80 calories per ounce (I use Kraft Light Naturals)
  Monterey Jack with jalapeño peppers—110 calories per ounce (I use Kraft Casino)
  mozzarella—80 calories per ounce (I use Kraft)
  Swiss, reduced-fat—80 calories per ounce (I use Kraft Light Naturals)

Chow Mein Noodles: 150 calories per ½ cup (I use La Choy)

Cooking Spray, Low-Calorie (All Flavors): 2 calories per serving (I use Pam)

Cottage Cheese, Low-Fat (1 Percent Fat): 80 calories per four-ounce serving (I use Light 'n' Lively)

Cream Cheese, Whipped, Light: 60 calories per ounce (I use Philadelphia Light)

Evaporated Skim Milk: 100 calories per ½ cup (I use Carnation)

Gelatin, Sugar-Free (All Flavors, Prepared): 8 calories per ½ cup (I use Jell-O)

Ginger Ale, Diet: less than 1 calorie per cup (I use Shasta)

Grape Soda, Diet: less than 1 calorie per cup (I use Shasta)

Margarine, Low-Calorie: 50 calories per tablespoon (I use Kraft Touch of Butter)

Mayonnaise, Low-Calorie: 45 calories per tablespoon (I use Kraft Light)

Orange Marmalade: 18 calories per teaspoon (I use Smucker's)

Picante Sauce: 1½ calories per teaspoon (I use Pace)

Raspberry Spread, Low-Calorie: 8 calories per teaspoon (I use Weight Watchers)

Rice, Wild-and-White Blend (Prepared Without Margarine):   83 calories per ½ cup (I use Uncle Ben's Long Grain and Wild Rice with Herb Seasonings)

Salad Dressing: *oil-free Italian*—4 calories per tablespoon (I use Kraft)

   Catalina, reduced-calorie—16 calories per tablespoon (I use Kraft Free)

   dried Ranch, reduced-calorie (made with buttermilk and low-calorie mayonnaise)—20 calories per tablespoon (I use Hidden Valley Ranch)

Soup, Condensed (Cream of Celery, Cream of Chicken, and Cream of Mushroom):   100 calories per ½ cup (I use Campbell's)

Soup, Dried (Onion):   120 calories per package (I use Lipton)

Soy Sauce, Lite: 11 calories per tablespoon (I use Kikkoman Lite)

Turkey Ham: 36 calories per ounce (I use Hormel)

Yogurt: *plain, nonfat*—120 calories per 8-ounce serving (I use Dannon)

   flavored, low-fat—240 calories per 8-ounce serving (I use Dannon)

4
❧ SALADS ❧

TANGY CRANBERRY FIESTA SALAD

A delightfully tart blend of fruits and gelatin, this salad is especially delicious when paired with Roasted Chicken Breasts (see Index).

½ medium-sized orange, unpeeled
    and cut into chunks
¾ cup raw cranberries
½ cup chopped fresh strawberries
2 teaspoons sugar
1 3-ounce package sugar-free
    mixed-fruit gelatin
⅔ cup boiling water
¼ cup unsweetened pineapple
    juice
1 teaspoon grated orange zest
¼ cup cold water
4 ice cubes
Garnish: Lettuce leaves

1. Place orange chunks, cranberries, and strawberries in a food processor fitted with the steel blade or a blender. Blend thoroughly.

2. In a glass bowl, combine sugar, gelatin, and boiling water. Stir until sugar and gelatin are completely dissolved. Remove from heat and add juice, zest, cold water, and ice cubes. Stir until ice cubes have completely melted. Pour into the food processor or blender. Blend fruit and gelatin mixtures together.

3. Pour into four individual 6-ounce gelatin molds and chill until mixture is set (about two hours). Remove salads from molds (see note) and serve on a bed of crisp lettuce.

Serves 4
Approximately 0.1 gram fat per serving

Note: To remove gelatin from molds, dip the bottoms briefly into hot water before inverting.

ORANGE-KIWI GINGER

Fresh oranges, kiwi, and ginger ale give this gelatin salad a distinctively zesty taste.

1 3-ounce package sugar-free
  orange gelatin
1 cup boiling water
1 cup cold diet ginger ale
1 teaspoon fresh lemon juice
6 ice cubes
⅔ cup peeled orange sections
2 kiwis, peeled and cut into 8
  wedges each

1. Dissolve gelatin in boiling water. Add ginger ale, lemon juice, and ice cubes. Stir until ice melts and chill until very thick (about 10 minutes).

2. Whip mixture, with an electric mixer or in a food processor fitted with the steel blade, until fluffy and doubled in volume. Using a spoon, stir in orange sections. Pour mixture into four individual 6-ounce gelatin molds. Chill until mixture is very firm.

3. Remove gelatin from molds (see note) and place on decorative plates. Arrange 4 kiwi wedges around the base of each gelatin.

Serves 4
Approximately 0.03 gram fat per serving

Note: To remove gelatin from molds, dip the bottoms briefly into hot water before inverting.

BOUNTIFULLY LAYERED SALAD

This gelatin salad is sweet and creamy, with a hint of tropical fruit.

1 3-ounce package sugar-free lemon gelatin
1 3-ounce package sugar-free raspberry gelatin
2 cups boiling water
¾ cup cold water
1 teaspoon fresh lemon juice
½ cup plain nonfat yogurt
¼ teaspoon vanilla extract
½ cup undrained canned crushed pineapple in its own juice
Garnish: Lettuce leaves

1. Dissolve lemon gelatin in 1 cup of the boiling water. Refrigerate for 15 minutes.

2. In a separate bowl, dissolve raspberry gelatin in 1 cup boiling water. Add cold water and lemon juice and stir.

3. Pour half of the raspberry gelatin mixture into four individual 6-ounce molds *or* one 8-inch square pan. Refrigerate. Set aside the remaining raspberry gelatin mixture (do not refrigerate this).

4. Remove lemon gelatin from refrigerator. Add yogurt and vanilla extract. Blend well and refrigerate until mixture has thickened slightly. Pour in even amounts onto raspberry gelatin.

5. Add pineapple to reserved raspberry gelatin. Refrigerate until mixture has thickened slightly. Pour onto chilled gelatin (in even amounts). Chill until firm (about 2 hours).

6. To serve, remove gelatins from molds (see note) or, if using a pan, cut gelatin into 4 uniformly sized squares. Remove squares from pan and place each on a bed of crisp lettuce.

Serves 4
Approximately 0.1 gram fat per serving

Note: To remove gelatin from molds, dip the bottoms briefly into hot water before inverting.

SPICY PEACHES

Spiced peaches in an orange gelatin make for an especially delicious complement to almost any casserole.

1 17-ounce can sliced peaches in
   their own juice
2 tablespoons cider vinegar
12 cloves
1/8 teaspoon ground cinnamon
Dash ground allspice
1/2 cup water
1 3-ounce package sugar-free
   orange gelatin
10 ice cubes

1. Drain peaches, reserving juice, and chop peaches. In a saucepan, combine juice, vinegar, cloves, cinnamon, and allspice. Bring mixture to a boil. Add peaches and simmer for 10 minutes.

2. Remove cloves from mixture and discard. Add water and gelatin, stirring until gelatin is dissolved. Add ice cubes and stir until ice is melted. Pour mixture into a glass bowl and chill until set (about 1 hour).

Serves 4
Approximately 0.1 gram fat per serving

A FAMILY REUNION SALAD

This creamy gelatin, topped with a colorful array of fresh fruit, is very attractive when served in a decorative clear glass bowl.

1 3-ounce package sugar-free
   orange gelatin
1 cup boiling water
3/4 cup cold water
1 tablespoon fresh lemon juice
4 ice cubes
3 tablespoons "light" cream
   cheese
1/2 cup fresh peach slices
1/4 cup fresh pineapple chunks
1/4 cup pitted fresh dark sweet
   cherries

1. Mix gelatin with boiling water and stir until dissolved. Add cold water, lemon juice, and ice cubes. Stir until ice is melted.

2. Add cream cheese. Using an electric mixer, beat until cream cheese is well blended. Pour mixture into a decorative bowl and chill until firm (about 1 hour).

3. Arrange peach slices in a fan shape on top of gelatin to form an outer circle. Next, add an inner ring of pineapple chunks and, in the center, a mound of cherries.

Serves 4
Approximately 1.8 grams fat per serving

CARIBBEAN FRUIT SALAD

Tropical fruits with a creamy, double-sweet sauce.

¾ cup fresh pineapple chunks
½ cup peeled mango chunks
¼ cup banana slices
½ cup fresh strawberry slices
¼ cup low-fat piña colada or
  vanilla yogurt
½ teaspoon powdered sugar

1. In a decorative clear glass bowl, layer pineapple, mango, banana, and strawberry pieces.
2. Combine yogurt and powdered sugar, blending until smooth. Spoon over fruit.

Serves 4
Approximately 0.4 gram fat per serving

Variation: Replace the mango with 1 cup honeydew or cantaloupe chunks.

RASPBERRY-GLAZED PEACHES

This salad is best when served immediately after it's prepared because the hot raspberry glaze quickly soaks into the peaches, losing its distinctive flavor.

2 cups fresh peach slices
2 tablespoons plus 2 teaspoons
  low-calorie raspberry spread
1 tablespoon plus 1 teaspoon
  unsweetened apple juice

1. Arrange ½ cup of the peach slices decoratively on each of four individual salad plates.
2. In a small saucepan, combine raspberry spread and apple juice. Heat and stir until mixture is smooth (do *not* boil).
3. Drizzle 1 tablespoon glaze over each salad. Serve immediately.

Serves 4
Approximately 0.1 gram fat per serving

FRUITED MELON WEDGES

A cool, tempting salad of marinated fruit over cantaloupe is a light beginning to a refreshing summer meal.

1 5-inch cantaloupe
½ cup fresh strawberry slices
½ cup halved and pitted fresh dark
  sweet cherries
1 tablespoon frozen orange juice
  concentrate
¼ teaspoon grated orange zest
⅓ teaspoon (1 packet) Equal, if
  desired

1. Quarter and seed cantaloupe. Refrigerate quarters in an airtight container until chilled.

2. Combine strawberries, cherries, frozen juice, orange zest, and Equal. Toss well. Chill for at least 30 minutes.

3. To serve, place cantaloupe wedges on individual salad plates. Spoon ¼ cup fruit mixture onto the center of each wedge.

Serves 4
Approximately 0.3 gram fat per serving

HOT CURRIED FRUIT

Rich, sweet cooked fruit with spices is a tasty alternative to cold salads, especially on chilly nights.

½ cup peeled fresh peach chunks
½ cup fresh pineapple chunks
½ cup undrained canned apricots
  in their own juice
½ cup peeled apple slices
1 tablespoon dark brown sugar,
  not packed
½ teaspoon curry powder
¼ teaspoon ground cinnamon
¼ teaspoon vanilla extract
⅓ teaspoon (1 packet) Equal

1. Preheat oven to 350°F.

2. Combine all ingredients in a heatproof dish. Blend well.

3. Tightly cover dish and bake for 20 to 25 minutes or until pineapple is tender. Serve immediately.

Serves 4
Approximately 0.2 gram fat per serving

GINGERED FRUIT KABOBS

A refreshing way to serve summer's sweetest fruits.

1 cup fresh strawberries
1½ cups watermelon cubes or balls
1 cup honeydew cubes or balls
1 cup diet ginger ale
4-5 drops fresh lemon juice
Garnish: Lettuce leaves

1. Thread an equal amount of each fruit on eight 6-inch bamboo skewers, alternating the strawberries, watermelon, and honeydew. Chill until serving time.
2. Just before serving, pour ginger ale over fruit. Sprinkle with lemon juice and place kabobs on a bed of crisp lettuce to serve.

Serves 4
Approximately 0.5 gram fat per serving

WALDORF SALAD

Fruit, celery, and nuts tossed with a sweet, creamy sauce.

1 cup chopped celery
1 cup chopped apple
1 tablespoon halved raisins
1 tablespoon walnut pieces, toasted (see note)
3 tablespoons plain nonfat yogurt
⅓ teaspoon (1 packet) Equal

1. In a small bowl, combine celery, apple, raisins, and walnut pieces.
2. In a separate bowl, blend yogurt and Equal. Pour over salad ingredients and toss lightly. Refrigerate for 30 minutes to allow flavors to blend.

Serves 4
Approximately 1.1 grams fat per serving

Note: To toast walnuts, simply cook them under the broiler until the pieces begin to brown. Walnuts toast quickly, so watch them carefully to prevent burning.

EUROPE'S PRIDE

A beautiful blend of tastes from Italy, France, and Greece.

2 tablespoons dry white wine
1 tablespoon fresh lemon juice
1 tablespoon chopped fresh
   parsley
1½ teaspoons olive oil
¾ teaspoon dried oregano leaves
⅛ teaspoon garlic powder
⅛ teaspoon ground cumin
1 ounce hard salami
3 cups torn leaf lettuce
1 tablespoon plus 1½ teaspoons
   crumbled feta cheese
2 tablespoons chopped red onion
Salt and pepper to taste

1. In a small bowl or jar, mix together wine, lemon juice, parsley, olive oil, oregano, garlic powder, and cumin. If time allows, refrigerate dressing for 2 to 3 hours to let the flavors blend.
2. When ready to serve, cut salami into paper-thin strips. Combine salami, lettuce, cheese, and onion in a salad bowl. Pour dressing over salad ingredients and toss well. Sprinkle salad with salt and pepper if desired. Serve immediately.

Serves 4
Approximately 3.6 grams fat per serving

MARINATED MUSHROOMS WITH BLUE CHEESE

Fresh vine-ripened tomatoes topped with mushrooms marinated in a blue cheese dressing make a flavorful summer salad.

2 teaspoons packed blue cheese
⅓ cup oil-free Italian dressing
2 tablespoons finely chopped red
   onion
½ pound fresh mushrooms,
   cleaned and quartered
Salt and pepper to taste
4 medium-sized tomatoes

1. Using a food processor fitted with the steel blade or a blender, combine cheese, salad dressing, and onion, blending thoroughly.
2. Pour mixture over mushrooms and toss gently but thoroughly. Sprinkle with salt and pepper if desired. Cover and marinate for at least 1 hour or overnight, stirring occasionally.
3. Just before serving, slice tomatoes ½ inch thick. Arrange tomato slices on four individual salad plates. Top each with one-quarter of the marinated mushrooms. Serve immediately.

Serves 4
Approximately 1.7 grams fat per serving

OLD-FASHIONED COLESLAW

This colorful blend of vegetables is reminiscent of the coleslaw my family used to serve at picnics and get-togethers. If you prefer, you can use 3½ cups green cabbage and omit the red, but I think the two colors make for a very colorful salad.

2 cups finely shredded green
  cabbage
1½ cups finely shredded red
  cabbage
2 tablespoons finely chopped
  green bell pepper
2 tablespoons finely chopped red
  onion
½ stalk celery, chopped
1 carrot, shredded
3 tablespoons white vinegar
⅔ teaspoon (2 packets) Equal
¼ teaspoon dry mustard
⅛ teaspoon pepper
½ teaspoon salt, if desired

In a large bowl, combine all ingredients and mix well. Cover bowl and refrigerate for at least 3 hours or overnight.

Serves 4
Approximately 1 gram fat per serving

CREAMY CUCUMBERS

A creamy onion and horseradish dressing gives these cucumbers a zesty, flavorful taste.

2 medium-sized cucumbers,
  peeled if desired
2 tablespoons plus 2 teaspoons
  low-calorie mayonnaise
1 tablespoon plus 1 teaspoon plain
  nonfat yogurt
2 teaspoons prepared horseradish
2 teaspoons finely chopped red or
  white onion
¼ teaspoon dry mustard
Salt and pepper to taste

1. Cut cucumbers into ⅛-inch slices and blot dry.
2. In a mixing bowl, combine mayonnaise, yogurt, horseradish, onion, mustard, and salt and pepper. Blend well.
3. Pour mixture over cucumber slices. Toss together and serve immediately.

Serves 4
Approximately 3.3 grams fat per serving

THE STACKED SALAD

A rich, crispy, flavor-blended salad that tastes exactly like the popular calorie-rich version.

3½ cups torn leaf lettuce
¼ cup shredded red cabbage
2 tablespoons finely chopped red
    onion
3 tablespoons frozen peas, thawed
⅓ cup Ranch dressing (see below)
Salt and pepper to taste
3 tablespoons finely grated
    reduced-fat cheddar cheese
1 bacon strip, broiled crisp,
    blotted dry, and crumbled

Ranch Dressing
1 1.1-ounce package dried
    reduced-calorie Ranch dressing
    mix
½ cup low-calorie mayonnaise
1½ cups buttermilk

1. In a decorative glass bowl, layer lettuce, cabbage, onion, and peas.
2. Spoon dressing evenly over layered vegetables. Sprinkle with salt and pepper if desired. Cover bowl and refrigerate for at least 3 hours. Sprinkle salad with cheese and bacon, and serve.

To Make Dressing
  Combine all ingredients in a bowl that has a tight-fitting lid. Cover and refrigerate for at least 30 minutes before using.

Serves 5
Approximately 3.8 grams fat per serving

FROM A CORNER OF CHINATOWN

Crisp water chestnuts and chow mein noodles make for a unique and refreshing Oriental salad.

3½ cups torn leaf lettuce
¼ cup well-drained sliced water
    chestnuts
2 tablespoons frozen peas, thawed
1 scallion, diagonally sliced ½ inch
    thick
⅓ cup Chinatown Soy salad
    dressing (see Index)
3 tablespoons crispy chow mein
    noodles

1. Combine lettuce, water chestnuts, peas, and scallion in a salad bowl.
2. Pour salad dressing over vegetables and toss well. Top salad with chow mein noodles. Toss again, if desired, and serve immediately.

Serves 4
Approximately 1 gram fat per serving

MANDARIN SALAD WITH ALMONDS

Toasted almonds enhance the flavor of this slightly sweet salad. If desired, ¼ cup sliced fresh strawberries may be substituted for the mandarin oranges called for here.

4 cups fresh spinach leaves, thoroughly washed and blotted dry

2 tablespoons chopped scallion

¼ cup drained canned mandarin oranges in light syrup

1 tablespoon plus 2 teaspoons crumbled toasted almonds (see note)

8 small fresh mushrooms, cleaned and sliced thin

¼ cup Sweet Basil Vinaigrette salad dressing (see Index)

⅔ teaspoon (2 packets) Equal

1. In a serving bowl, combine spinach, scallion, oranges, almonds, and mushrooms.

2. In a separate bowl, combine salad dressing and Equal. Blend well and pour over salad. Toss gently but thoroughly. Serve immediately.

Serves 4
Approximately 3.1 grams fat per serving

Note: To toast almonds, simply cook them under the broiler until they have browned, watching them carefully to prevent burning.

LEMON-LIMED TOMATOES

A zesty way to serve garden-fresh tomatoes.

3 medium-sized vine-ripened tomatoes

Juice of 2 medium-sized lemons

Juice of 2 medium-sized limes

Salt and freshly ground pepper to taste

3 tablespoons chopped fresh parsley

1. Cut tomatoes into thin slices and arrange on a serving platter.

2. Drizzle lemon and lime juice over tomatoes and add salt and pepper. Sprinkle with parsley.

3. Let salad stand for 10 minutes before serving.

Serves 4
Approximately 0.3 gram fat per serving

CORN MEDLEY

A creamy, cold vegetable toss with a delightful summer crispness.

1 medium-sized tomato, seeded
  and chopped
¼ medium-sized green or red bell
  pepper, chopped
2 tablespoons chopped red onion
½ medium-sized cucumber, peeled
  and chopped
2 tablespoons buttermilk
1 tablespoon low-calorie
  mayonnaise
½ teaspoon salt
⅛ teaspoon celery seed
⅛ teaspoon dry mustard
¼ teaspoon freshly ground black
  pepper
1 cup unthawed frozen corn
  kernels

1. In a small bowl, combine tomato, bell pepper, onion, and cucumber.

2. In a separate bowl, combine buttermilk, mayonnaise, salt, celery seed, mustard, and pepper. Mix well and pour over vegetables. Toss thoroughly.

3. Just before serving, toss mixture with frozen corn. Serve immediately.

Serves 4
Approximately 1.5 grams fat per serving

CARROT AND BELL PEPPER SALAD

This sweet-and-sour marinated salad is extremely easy to prepare and is delicious with poultry and pork dishes.

2 cups sliced carrots
½ medium-sized red onion, sliced
  thin
½ medium-sized green bell
  pepper, sliced thin
¼ cup reduced-calorie Catalina
  salad dressing
⅓ teaspoon (1 packet) Equal
1½ teaspoons cider vinegar
1 teaspoon dry mustard

1. Steam carrots until tender but still slightly crisp. Refrigerate for 20 minutes or until chilled.

2. Place carrots, onion, and bell pepper in a glass bowl. Set aside.

3. Mix together salad dressing, Equal, vinegar, and mustard. Pour over vegetables and toss together. Refrigerate salad for at least 2 hours. Toss again before serving.

Serves 4
Approximately 0.1 gram fat per serving

A FRIEND'S GREEN CHILI SALAD

South-of-the-border-style tomatoes and crisp, fresh vegetables.

¼ cup (2 ounces) well drained
 canned chopped green chilies
6 medium-sized pitted black
 olives, sliced thin
2 tablespoons chopped scallion
 tops
¼ cup chopped celery
Salt and pepper to taste
2 medium-sized tomatoes
1 tablespoon plain nonfat yogurt
1 tablespoon low-calorie
 mayonnaise
Garnish: Chili powder

1. In a mixing bowl, combine chilies, olives, scallion tops, and celery. Toss together and add salt and pepper to taste.

2. Cut each tomato into four uniformly sized slices. Place 1 tablespoon of vegetable mixture on each tomato slice.

3. Blend together yogurt and mayonnaise. Spoon ¾ teaspoon of this mixture over each tomato slice. Sprinkle each slice lightly with chili powder and serve.

Serves 4
Approximately 2 grams fat per serving

SUMMER'S CUCUMBERS

A light, crunchy, and flavorful salad.

2 medium-sized cucumbers
½ medium-sized red onion
¾ cup water
½ cup cider vinegar
1 tablespoon sugar
⅔ teaspoon (2 packets) Equal
2 teaspoons vegetable oil
¼ teaspoon salt
⅛ teaspoon pepper

1. Peel cucumbers, if desired, and cut into thin slices. Cut onion into thin rings.

2. In a small mixing bowl or jar, combine water, vinegar, sugar, Equal, vegetable oil, salt, and pepper. Mix well.

3. Pour dressing over cucumber and onion slices. Refrigerate for at least 30 minutes.

Serves 4
Approximately 2.3 grams fat per serving

GARDEN AND PASTA SALAD

A delicious blend of marinated vegetables and pasta, tossed together with crisp lettuce leaves.

2 drained canned artichoke hearts
⅓ cup cooked spiral or corkscrew noodles
⅓ cup asparagus pieces, lightly steamed (if canned, well drained)
½ cup sliced fresh mushrooms
2 tablespoons finely chopped red onion
2 tablespoons finely chopped green bell pepper
½ teaspoon cider vinegar
¼ cup plus 1 tablespoon Italian's Italian salad dressing (see Index)
3 cups torn leaf lettuce

1. Cut each artichoke heart into eight pieces.
2. In a glass serving bowl, combine all ingredients except lettuce. Marinate in the refrigerator for 30 minutes.
3. Just before serving, toss lettuce with other salad ingredients. Serve immediately.

Serves 4
Approximately 1.8 grams fat per serving

SPECIAL DRESSINGS FOR SIMPLE SALADS

SWEET HONEY MUSTARD DRESSING

A flavorful mustard blended with honey and ginger. Use 2 tablespoons dressing with 1 cup lettuce and 1 tablespoon chopped red onion for each 50-calorie salad.

½ cup cold water
1 tablespoon cornstarch
⅓ cup Dijon mustard
⅓ cup honey
½ teaspoon ground ginger

1. In a small saucepan, combine water and cornstarch. Heat until mixture comes to a full boil. Boil for 1 minute, stirring occasionally. Remove mixture from heat, let cool slightly, and refrigerate for 10 minutes.

2. Mix mustard, honey, and ginger into cooled cornstarch mixture. Blend well and refrigerate for at least 30 minutes before serving.

3. To store, refrigerate in a covered jar or an airtight container.

Makes 1¼ cups
23 calories per tablespoon
Approximately 0.2 gram fat per salad serving

CHINATOWN SOY

A light, sweet, Oriental-flavored dressing. Use 2 tablespoons dressing with 1 cup lettuce, ¼ tomato, and 1 tablespoon chopped red onion for each 50-calorie salad.

1 cup cold water
1 tablespoon cornstarch
¼ cup "lite" soy sauce
¼ cup dark brown sugar (not packed)
3 tablespoons cider vinegar
2 tablespoons minced red or white onion
2 teaspoons vegetable oil
¼ teaspoon ground ginger
¼ teaspoon garlic powder

1. In a small saucepan, combine water and cornstarch. Heat until mixture comes to a full boil. Boil for 1 minute, stirring occasionally. Remove mixture from heat, cool slightly, and refrigerate for 10 minutes.

2. Mix soy sauce, brown sugar, vinegar, onion, vegetable oil, ginger, and garlic powder into cooled cornstarch mixture. Blend well and refrigerate for at least 30 minutes.

3. To store, refrigerate in a covered jar or an airtight container.

Makes 1½ cups
16 calories per tablespoon
Approximately 0.7 gram fat per salad serving

SIMPLY BLUE

This zesty dressing has all the tangy flavor of blue cheese, but it's much more refreshing than its heavier salad dressing cousin. Use 2 tablespoons dressing with 1 cup lettuce, ¼ tomato, and 1 tablespoon chopped red onion for each 50-calorie salad.

1 tablespoon packed (not crumbled) blue cheese
½ cup oil-free Italian dressing
1 tablespoon finely chopped red onion

1. Place cheese, Italian dressing, and onion in a food processor fitted with the steel blade or a blender. Blend thoroughly.

2. To store, refrigerate in a covered jar or an airtight container.

Makes ½ cup
16 calories per tablespoon
Approximately 0.2 gram fat per salad serving

Note: The flavor of this dressing is greatly enhanced if the dressing is refrigerated overnight.

CREAMY AVOCADO DRESSING

Somewhat reminiscent of a zesty guacamole, this is a unique and tasty way to top a salad. Use 2 tablespoons dressing with 1 cup lettuce, ¼ tomato, and 1 tablespoon chopped red onion for each 50-calorie salad.

1 large ripe avocado
3 tablespoons fresh lemon juice
2 tablespoons water
1 teaspoon prepared mustard
¼ teaspoon salt
¼ teaspoon black pepper
2–3 drops hot sauce
1 medium-sized tomato, chopped
   coarse
3 tablespoons finely chopped red
   onion

1. Peel and pit avocado and cut into chunks. Place avocado, lemon juice, water, mustard, salt, pepper, and hot sauce in a food processor fitted with the steel blade or a blender. Blend until smooth.

2. Transfer mixture to a mixing bowl. Add tomato and onion and mix dressing with a fork. Refrigerate for at least 1 hour before serving.

3. To store, refrigerate in a covered jar or an airtight container.

Makes 2 cups
13 calories per tablespoon
Approximately 1.5 grams fat per salad serving

ITALIAN'S ITALIAN

A delicately herbed oil and vinegar dressing. Use 2 tablespoons dressing with 1 cup lettuce, ¼ tomato, and 1 tablespoon chopped red onion for each 50-calorie salad.

1 cup cold water
1 tablespoon cornstarch
2 tablespoons plus 1 teaspoon red
   wine vinegar
2 tablespoons vegetable oil
1 tablespoon water
1 teaspoon salt
½ teaspoon dried oregano leaves
½ teaspoon garlic powder
½ teaspoon dry mustard

1. In a small saucepan, combine 1 cup water and cornstarch. Heat mixture until it comes to a full boil. Boil for 1 minute, stirring occasionally. Remove mixture from heat, cool slightly, and refrigerate for 10 minutes.

2. Mix vinegar, vegetable oil, 1 tablespoon water, salt, oregano, garlic powder, and dry mustard into cornstarch mixture. Blend well. Refrigerate for at least 30 minutes before serving.

3. To store, refrigerate in a covered jar or an airtight container.

Makes 1¼ cups
14 calories per tablespoon
Approximately 2.8 grams fat per salad serving

ZESTY LEMON VINAIGRETTE

This dressing has a rather intense, sophisticated taste that brightens up the flavor of almost any vegetable salad. Use 1 tablespoon plus 2 teaspoons dressing with 1 cup lettuce, ¼ tomato, and 1 tablespoon chopped red onion for each 50-calorie salad.

½ cup dry white wine
3 tablespoons fresh lemon juice
¼ cup chopped fresh parsley
2 tablespoons olive oil
1 tablespoon dried oregano leaves
½ teaspoon garlic powder
½ teaspoon ground cumin
¾ teaspoon salt
½ teaspoon pepper

1. In a mixing bowl, combine all ingredients, blending thoroughly. Refrigerate for at least 1 hour before serving.

2. To store, refrigerate in a covered jar or an airtight container.

Makes 1¼ cups
16 calories per tablespoon
Approximately 1.7 grams fat per salad serving

SWEET BASIL VINAIGRETTE

A hint of sweetness pervades this light herbed oil and vinegar dressing. Use 2 tablespoons dressing with 1 cup lettuce, ¼ tomato, and 1 tablespoon chopped red onion for each 50-calorie salad.

1 cup cold water
1 tablespoon cornstarch
2 tablespoons fresh lemon juice
2 tablespoons cider vinegar
2 tablespoons olive oil
½ teaspoon dried basil leaves
½ teaspoon dry mustard
¾ teaspoon sugar
½ teaspoon salt
¼ teaspoon pepper
¼ teaspoon garlic powder

1. In a small saucepan, combine water and cornstarch. Heat until mixture comes to a full boil. Boil for 1 minute, stirring occasionally. Remove mixture from heat, cool slightly, and refrigerate for 10 minutes.

2. Mix lemon juice, vinegar, olive oil, basil, dry mustard, sugar, salt, pepper, and garlic powder into cornstarch mixture, blending well. Refrigerate for at least 30 minutes before serving.

3. To store, refrigerate in a covered jar or an airtight container.

Makes 1¼ cups
15 calories per tablespoon
Approximately 2.8 grams fat per salad serving

SMOOTH AND CREAMY BLUE

Another variation on the usually fattening blue cheese salad dressing. This is a creamy version, full of zest and a hint of garlic. Use 1½ tablespoons dressing with 1 cup lettuce and 1 teaspoon chopped red onion for each 50-calorie salad.

½ cup plain nonfat yogurt
¼ cup crumbled (not packed) blue
   cheese
2 tablespoons low-calorie
   mayonnaise
¼ teaspoon black pepper
¼ teaspoon salt
⅛ teaspoon garlic powder

1. Place all ingredients in a food processor fitted with the steel blade or a blender. Blend thoroughly.

2. To store, refrigerate in a covered jar or an airtight container.

Makes ¾ cup
29 calories per tablespoon
Approximately 3.3 grams fat per salad serving

CREAMY GARLIC WITH PARMESAN

A delicately flavored garlic and onion dressing. Use 1 tablespoon plus 2 teaspoons dressing with 1 cup lettuce and ¼ tomato for each 50-calorie salad.

½ cup buttermilk
¼ cup low-calorie mayonnaise
2 tablespoons finely chopped
   white onion
1 teaspoon Dijon mustard
1 teaspoon fresh lemon juice
⅛ teaspoon white pepper
¼ teaspoon garlic powder
⅛ teaspoon salt
Freshly grated Parmesan cheese
   (1 teaspoon per serving)
Freshly ground black pepper, if
   desired

1. In a mixing bowl, combine all ingredients except Parmesan cheese. Mix well.

2. Just before serving, thoroughly toss dressing with salad. Sprinkle 1 teaspoon Parmesan cheese onto each salad serving. Top with freshly ground black pepper if desired.

3. To store, refrigerate in a covered jar or an airtight container.

Makes 1 cup
15 calories per tablespoon
Approximately 7 calories per teaspoon Parmesan cheese
Approximately 2.6 grams fat per salad serving

Variation: Creamy Garlic with Dill: Omit the Parmesan and mix in ½ teaspoon dried dill.

THOUSAND ISLAND DRESSING

A sweet, creamy, full-bodied dressing. Use 2 tablespoons dressing with 1 cup lettuce, ¼ tomato, and 1 tablespoon chopped red onion for each 50-calorie salad.

½ cup plain nonfat yogurt
⅓ cup low-calorie mayonnaise
¼ cup catsup or bottled chili sauce
3 tablespoons finely chopped red onion
1 tablespoon fresh lemon juice
¼ teaspoon Worcestershire sauce
⅛ teaspoon salt
Dash hot sauce
Dash freshly ground black pepper
¼ cup finely chopped celery

1. Combine all ingredients in a mixing bowl, blending thoroughly.
2. To store, refrigerate in a covered jar or an airtight container.

Makes 1½ cups
19 calories per tablespoon
Approximately 2.6 grams fat per salad serving

CREAMY DIJON

A smooth mustard dressing with just a bit of a bite. Use 2 tablespoons dressing with 1 cup lettuce, ¼ tomato, and 1 tablespoon chopped red onion for each 50-calorie salad.

½ cup cold water
1 tablespoon cornstarch
1 medium-sized egg
⅓ cup low-calorie mayonnaise
1 tablespoon cider vinegar
½ teaspoon salt
⅛ teaspoon pepper
1 tablespoon plus 2½ teaspoons Dijon mustard

1. In a small saucepan, combine water with cornstarch. Heat until mixture comes to a full boil. Boil for 1 minute, stirring occasionally. Remove mixture from heat, cool slightly, and refrigerate for 10 minutes.
2. In a blender, combine cornstarch mixture with all other ingredients and blend well. Refrigerate for at least 30 minutes before serving.
3. To store, refrigerate in a covered jar or an airtight container for up to 2 days.

Makes 1¼ cups
16 calories per tablespoon
Approximately 3.4 grams fat per salad serving

PLAIN AND SIMPLE 50-CALORIE SALADS

When there's just no time to create a more elaborate salad, these quick and easy alternatives can be a dieter's best friend.

Apples: ⅔ cup sliced equals one 50-calorie serving. For a bit of extra flavor, sprinkle ground cinnamon over the slices. Approximately 0.3 gram fat per serving.

Applesauce: ⅔ cup unsweetened equals one 50-calorie serving. Ground cinnamon sprinkled on top makes a nice garnish. Approximately 0.3 gram fat per serving.

Apricots: 2 small fresh *or* 3 medium-sized halves canned (packed in their own juice) equal one 50-calorie serving. Approximately 0.2 gram fat per serving.

Asparagus: 7 fresh or canned spears tossed with 2 tablespoons oil-free Italian salad dressing equal one 50-calorie serving. Note: Marinate salad for 20 minutes before serving. Approximately 0.3 gram fat per serving.

Blueberries: ⅔ cup fresh equals one 50-calorie serving. Approximately 0.4 gram fat per serving.

Cantaloupe: 1 cup cubed equals one 50-calorie serving. Approximately 0.1 gram fat per serving.

Cherries (Dark Sweet): 10 large fresh cherries equal one 50-calorie serving. Approximately 0.2 gram fat per serving.

Cucumber: ½ medium-sized sliced, tossed with 2½ tablespoons oil-free Italian salad dressing, equals one 50-calorie serving. Approximately 0.1 gram fat per serving.

Grapes (Red or White): ½ cup fresh equals one 50-calorie serving. Approximately 0.1 gram fat per serving.

Green Beans: 1½ cups canned or fresh steamed, tossed with 2½ tablespoons oil-free Italian salad dressing, equal one 50-calorie serving. Note: Marinate salad for 10 minutes before serving. Approximately 0.4 gram fat per serving.

Honeydew: 1 cup cubed equals one 50-calorie serving. Approximately 0.4 gram fat per serving.

Nectarines: 1 medium-sized sliced equals one 50-calorie serving. Approximately 0.1 gram fat per serving.

Oranges: ½ cup fresh sections equals one 50-calorie serving. Approximately 0.2 gram fat per serving.

Peaches: ¾ cup fresh slices equals one 50-calorie serving. Approximately 0.1 gram fat per serving.

Pears: ⅔ cup fresh slices equals one 50-calorie serving. Approximately 0.2 gram fat per serving.

Pineapple: ¾ cup fresh cubes *or* 1 slice canned in its own juice equals one 50-calorie serving. Approximately 0.2 gram fat per serving.

Raspberries (Red): ⅔ cup fresh equals one 50-calorie serving. Approximately 1.4 grams fat per serving.

Strawberries: 1 cup sliced fresh equals one 50-calorie serving. Approximately 0.8 gram fat per serving.

Tangerines: 2 small equal one 50-calorie serving. Approximately 0.2 gram fat per serving.

Tomatoes: 1½ medium-sized sliced equal one 50-calorie serving. Approximately 0.5 gram fat per serving.

Watermelon: 1 cup cubed equals one 50-calorie serving. Approximately 0.2 gram fat per serving.

5
MAIN COURSES
❧ POULTRY ❧

CHICKEN A L'ORANGE

Tender roasted chicken in a delicate, sweet orange sauce.

Low-calorie cooking spray
4 6-ounce skinless chicken breast
   halves
⅔ cup sliced yellow onion
¼ cup orange marmalade
¼ cup frozen orange juice
   concentrate
½ teaspoon grated orange zest

1. Preheat oven to 350°F.
2. Coat a nonstick skillet with low-calorie cooking spray. Heat skillet. Add chicken and onion and cook over medium-high heat, meat side down, for 2 to 3 minutes, until chicken is lightly browned and onions are slightly translucent. Transfer chicken to a baking dish and spoon onions over chicken.
3. In a small bowl, mix together marmalade, orange juice concentrate, and orange zest. Spoon 2 tablespoons over each chicken breast. Bake, uncovered, for 20 minutes.

Serves 4
Approximately 3.2 grams fat per serving

SUGGESTED ACCOMPANIMENTS (see Index)

Green salad with Sweet Honey Mustard Dressing
Cauliflower and Carrots with Nutmeg
Tropical Citrus Freeze

PEPPERED CHICKEN TERIYAKI

Easy-to-make yet elegant fare—heavily peppered, teriyaki-marinated chicken, served au jus over rice.

4 5½-ounce skinless chicken breast
   halves
¼ cup teriyaki sauce
Freshly ground black pepper
3 tablespoons water
2 cups hot cooked white rice (no
   margarine added during
   cooking)
Garnish: Chopped fresh parsley

1. Place chicken breasts and teriyaki sauce in an airtight container and refrigerate for 8 hours.
2. Preheat oven to 400°F.
3. Transfer chicken to a baking dish. Cover chicken with marinade and sprinkle again with pepper.
4. Bake, uncovered, for 15 minutes, basting chicken with marinade occasionally.
5. Add water to drippings and stir. Continue baking for 8 minutes more, basting chicken occasionally.
6. Spoon cooked rice onto a serving platter and arrange chicken around the outer edges of rice. Stir well and pour sauce over the entire dish. Garnish with parsley.

Serves 4
Approximately 3.5 grams fat per serving

SUGGESTED ACCOMPANIMENTS (see Index)

Carrot and Bell Pepper Salad
Fresh Broccoli and Ginger Oriental
Gingered Fruit in Plum Wine

MY ANNIE'S FAVORITE

A heavenly dark sweet cherry sauce covers this baked chicken.

4 7-ounce skinless chicken breast halves
Salt and pepper to taste
1 cup undrained canned dark sweet cherries in heavy syrup
¼ teaspoon ground ginger
2 teaspoons cornstarch

1. Preheat the broiler.
2. Place chicken on the rack of a broiling pan. Sprinkle with salt and pepper and place in the broiler, about 5 inches from the heat source. Broil for 6 to 8 minutes.
3. In a small saucepan, combine cherries, ginger, and cornstarch. Boil for 1 minute. Remove from heat.
4. Arrange chicken on a serving platter and spoon cherry sauce over each piece.

Serves 4
Approximately 4.3 grams fat per serving

SUGGESTED ACCOMPANIMENTS (see Index)

From a Corner of Chinatown
Fresh Broccoli and Ginger Oriental
Coconut Meringues with Pineapple Filling

CHICKEN WITH BLUE CHEESE

A rich blue cheese cream sauce serves as a delicious base for this flavorful chicken dish.

1⅓ cups canned or homemade
  chicken broth
1 cup skim milk
2 tablespoons flour
Low-calorie cooking spray
½ pound fresh mushrooms,
  cleaned and sliced
1⅔ cups cubed cooked chicken
  breast meat
½ cup frozen peas, thawed
1 2-ounce jar chopped pimiento,
  undrained
Salt and pepper to taste
6 slices "diet" bread
2 tablespoons crumbled blue
  cheese

1. In a medium-sized saucepan, combine broth, skim milk, and flour. Blend well and cook over medium-high heat until sauce has thickened.

2. Coat a nonstick skillet with low-calorie cooking spray. Heat skillet. Add mushrooms and sauté over medium-high heat for 2 to 3 minutes until browned. Transfer mushrooms to sauce and add chicken, peas, and pimiento. Heat thoroughly and add salt and pepper to taste.

3. Toast bread. Cut each slice into four triangles. On each of four individual dinner plates, arrange six toast points.

4. Just before serving, add blue cheese to chicken mixture, blending gently. Spoon mixture evenly over toast points and serve immediately.

Serves 4
Approximately 4 grams fat per serving

SUGGESTED ACCOMPANIMENTS (see Index)

Green salad with Zesty Lemon Vinaigrette
Brown-Buttered Asparagus
Frozen Sugar-Coated Grapes

CHICKEN SIZZLER

Richly browned chicken, seasoned and served sizzling hot in its own robust juices.

4 5¼-ounce skinless, boneless
  chicken breast halves
Low-calorie cooking spray
1 tablespoon plus 1 teaspoon olive
  oil
¾ teaspoon dried oregano leaves
Salt and freshly ground pepper to
  taste
1 tablespoon fresh lemon juice
2 tablespoons fresh lime juice
3 tablespoons water

1. Flatten chicken breasts to a ¼-inch thickness (see note).

2. Coat a fairly large skillet with low-calorie cooking spray. Add olive oil and heat skillet. Place chicken breasts in skillet. Sprinkle with ½ teaspoon of the oregano leaves, salt, and pepper. Cook over medium-high heat for about 7 minutes or until chicken is richly browned on both sides. Transfer chicken to a serving platter.

3. Add remaining oregano, lemon juice, lime juice, and water to pan drippings in skillet. Cook over medium heat for 2 minutes, scraping sides and bottom of skillet occasionally. Cover skillet and cook for 1 minute longer.

4. Immediately pour sauce over chicken pieces and serve.

Serves 4
Approximately 9.5 grams fat per serving

Note: To flatten chicken breasts, place one breast half between two sheets of wax paper and pound with a meat mallet, rolling pin, or heavy-bottomed pan, being careful not to tear chicken.

SUGGESTED ACCOMPANIMENTS (see Index)

Garden and Pasta Salad
Baked Mélange
Baked Pineapple and Bananas

OLD BAY CHICKEN
WITH BROCCOLI-RICE CASSEROLE

Old Bay seasoning, available in the spice section of supermarkets, is most commonly used with shellfish. Here it enhances baked chicken served with broccoli, rice, cheese, and a dash of chili powder.

Low-calorie cooking spray
4 7-ounce skinless chicken breast halves
Old Bay seasoning or Cajun seasoning to taste
1⅔ cups frozen chopped broccoli, steamed
¾ cup cooked white rice (no margarine added during cooking)
⅓ cup grated reduced-fat cheddar cheese
⅛ teaspoon chili powder
⅛ teaspoon garlic powder
Dash of cayenne pepper
Salt and pepper to taste
Paprika, if desired

1. Preheat oven to 350°F.
2. Coat a baking sheet with low-calorie cooking spray. Place chicken on sheet and sprinkle with Old Bay seasoning.
3. In a large bowl, combine broccoli, rice, cheese, chili powder, garlic powder, cayenne pepper, salt, and pepper. Transfer to a baking dish and sprinkle with paprika.
4. Tightly cover dish and place it and the chicken in the oven. Bake for 35 minutes or until chicken is thoroughly done.
5. Place broccoli-rice casserole in the center of a serving platter. Arrange chicken breasts around mixture and serve immediately.

Serves 4
Approximately 5.6 grams fat per serving

SUGGESTED ACCOMPANIMENTS (see Index)

Orange-Kiwi Ginger
The Grilled Onion
Banana Cream Supreme

BROILED CHICKEN BREASTS WITH HERBED VEGETABLE RICE

A luscious, lemony dish—tender chicken, rice, sweet red pepper, and flavorful seasonings.

½ teaspoon dried basil leaves
¼ teaspoon dried dill
¼ teaspoon dry mustard
¼ teaspoon garlic powder
¼ teaspoon salt
⅛ teaspoon black pepper
4 6-ounce skinless chicken breast halves
2 teaspoons olive oil
Juice of 1 medium-sized lemon
Low-calorie cooking spray
⅓ cup chopped red bell pepper
⅓ cup chopped celery
3 tablespoons chopped yellow onion
1½ teaspoons chicken bouillon granules
3 tablespoons hot water
1⅔ cups hot cooked white rice (no margarine added during cooking)
2 tablespoons chopped fresh parsley
Dash cayenne pepper
Dash garlic powder
Salt and pepper to taste

1. Mix together basil, dill, mustard, garlic powder, ¼ teaspoon salt, and ⅛ teaspoon black pepper.

2. Brush chicken breasts with olive oil and place in a shallow dish. Drizzle lemon juice over chicken. Top with herb mixture and refrigerate for at least 30 minutes and up to 8 hours.

3. Preheat the broiler. Place chicken on the rack of a broiling pan. Broil, about 5 inches below the heat source, for 5 minutes or until chicken is thoroughly cooked.

4. While chicken is cooking, coat a nonstick skillet with low-calorie cooking spray. Add bell pepper, celery, and onion. Sauté over medium-high heat for 1 to 2 minutes until onion is translucent.

5. In a small bowl, combine bouillon granules and hot water. Add to vegetables. Mix in rice, parsley, cayenne pepper, garlic powder, and salt and pepper to taste.

6. Mound rice on a serving platter and arrange chicken breasts around rice. Serve immediately.

Serves 4
Approximately 5.5 grams fat per serving

SUGGESTED ACCOMPANIMENTS (see Index)

Green salad with Creamy Dijon
Baked Tomatoes with Cheese
Strawberries with Minted Chocolate

BARBECUED CHICKEN BREASTS

An all-American dish, perfect for summer grills and sunny days.

Low-calorie cooking spray
½ cup "lite" catsup
⅓ cup plus 1 tablespoon water
2 tablespoons finely chopped
  yellow onion
2 tablespoons red wine vinegar
1 tablespoon dark brown sugar
  (not packed)
1 teaspoon chili powder
1 teaspoon prepared mustard
1 teaspoon Worcestershire sauce
⅛ teaspoon hot sauce
⅛ teaspoon salt
1 medium-sized clove garlic,
  minced
4 8-ounce skinless chicken breast
  halves

1. Coat a broiling pan (or the rack of a grill) with low-calorie cooking spray. If you are preparing this recipe in the oven, preheat the broiler. If you are using a grill, preheat it or light the charcoal.

2. In a saucepan, combine all ingredients except chicken. Bring to a boil, then reduce heat and simmer, uncovered, for 5 minutes. Remove from heat.

3. If broiling, place chicken under the broiler, about 5 inches from the heat source. Baste with sauce. Broil 8 to 10 minutes or until chicken is thoroughly done. Be sure to turn chicken over at least once and baste frequently while it is cooking. If using a grill, cook chicken 30 to 35 minutes, basting and turning every 5 minutes until chicken is thoroughly cooked.

Serves 4
Approximately 5 grams fat per serving

SUGGESTED ACCOMPANIMENTS (see Index)

Corn Medley
All-American Oven Fries
My Willie's Apples

BROILED SPICY MUSTARD CHICKEN

This easy-to-make dish gets its rich flavor from a tangy tarragon–hot mustard sauce.

Low-calorie cooking spray
¼ cup Dijon mustard
Juice of 1 medium-sized lime
½ teaspoon dried tarragon leaves
Hot sauce to taste
4 8-ounce skinless chicken breast
   halves

1. Preheat the broiler. Coat a broiling pan with low-calorie cooking spray.

2. Mix together mustard, lime juice, tarragon, and hot sauce. Brush mixture on chicken. Place chicken on the rack of the broiling pan and broil, about 5 inches from the heat source, for 8 to 10 minutes or until chicken is thoroughly done. Be sure to turn chicken over at least once and baste again with sauce.

Serves 4
Approximately 5.6 grams fat per serving

SUGGESTED ACCOMPANIMENTS (see Index)

Caribbean Fruit Salad
Dilled Oven Fries
Dropped Strawberries

CHICKEN BURGUNDY

Lightly floured and browned chicken with a rich, hearty burgundy sauce and melted mozzarella.

4 4-ounce skinless, boneless
   chicken breast halves
2 tablespoons flour
Low-calorie cooking spray
1 tablespoon olive oil
Salt and pepper to taste
Paprika to taste
Garlic powder to taste
½ pound fresh mushrooms, sliced
¼ cup chopped scallion tops
½ cup burgundy
⅓ cup canned or homemade beef
   broth
½ cup shredded mozzarella cheese

1. Preheat oven to 350°F.
2. Flatten each piece of chicken to a ⅛-inch thickness (see note). Lightly sprinkle flour over both sides of each chicken piece.
3. Coat a nonstick skillet with low-calorie cooking spray. Add oil and turn heat to medium-high. When oil is hot, add chicken and brown each side for 3 to 4 minutes.
4. Place chicken in a baking dish. Add salt, pepper, paprika, and garlic powder to taste.
5. Add mushrooms and scallions to pan drippings in skillet. Cook over medium heat until scallions become slightly translucent. Spoon mushrooms and scallions over chicken, keeping the pan drippings in the skillet. Add wine and broth to skillet and heat, scraping the sides of the pan often. Reduce heat and simmer sauce for 2 minutes; then add salt and pepper to taste.
6. Pour sauce over chicken and sprinkle cheese on top. Bake for 8 to 10 minutes or until chicken is thoroughly done. To give the chicken an even richer appearance, place it under the broiler, about 5 inches away from the heat source, and broil for 1 minute.
7. Transfer chicken to a serving platter and spoon sauce over all pieces.

Serves 4
Approximately 8.3 grams fat per serving

Note: To flatten chicken breasts, place one breast half between two sheets of wax paper and pound with a meat mallet, rolling pin, or heavy-bottomed pan, being careful not to tear chicken.

SUGGESTED ACCOMPANIMENTS (see Index)

Europe's Pride
Broccoli with Delicate Mustard Sauce
Chocolate Crumb "Crème de Menthe"

CHICKEN DIJON

An elegant dish, seasoned with white wine and herbs and accompanied by a rich mustard cream sauce.

Low-calorie cooking spray
4 7-ounce skinless chicken breast
  halves
1½ cups dry white wine
¼ teaspoon dried tarragon leaves
¼ teaspoon dried chervil leaves
½ teaspoon salt
¼ teaspoon pepper
2–3 drops hot sauce
2 medium-sized egg yolks
2 tablespoons Dijon mustard
2 tablespoons plain nonfat yogurt
Dash cayenne pepper
2 tablespoons flour

1. Coat a nonstick skillet with low-calorie cooking spray. Heat skillet. Add chicken, meat side down, and cook over medium-high heat until browned (about 3 minutes). Add wine, tarragon, chervil, salt, and pepper. Cover skillet, reduce heat, and simmer for 35 minutes. Remove chicken from sauce and place on a heated platter to keep it warm.

2. Mix hot sauce into egg yolks and blend. Add mustard, yogurt, and cayenne pepper and cook over medium-high heat, stirring briskly and constantly. Just before sauce comes to a boil, reduce heat, add flour, and stir until sauce has thickened. (Do not let sauce come to a boil at any time.)

3. Pour sauce over chicken pieces and serve immediately.

Serves 4
Approximately 6.7 grams fat per serving

SUGGESTED ACCOMPANIMENTS (see Index)

The Stacked Salad
Baked Cloved Onions
Light Crepes with Apples and Cinnamon Sugar

CHICKEN AND BROCCOLI ORIENTAL

To make this dish even easier to prepare, use precut vegetables from your local grocer's salad bar.

Low-calorie cooking spray
½ pound skinless, boneless chicken breast, cut into bite-sized pieces
1 tablespoon vegetable oil
4 cups broccoli flowerets
1 cup coarsely chopped green cabbage
1 cup diagonally sliced celery
1 cup sliced yellow onion
¼ pound fresh mushrooms, sliced
1 8-ounce can bamboo shoots, thoroughly drained
1 8-ounce can sliced water chestnuts, thoroughly drained
2 cups water
2 tablespoons cornstarch
¼ cup "lite" soy sauce
2 tablespoons chicken bouillon granules
2 teaspoons sugar
½ teaspoon garlic powder
2½ cups hot cooked white rice (no margarine added during cooking)

1. Coat a wok with low-calorie cooking spray and heat.
2. Place chicken in wok and stir-fry over medium-high heat for about 2 minutes or until cooked. Remove chicken and set aside.
3. Heat oil in wok. Add broccoli, cabbage, celery, onion, mushrooms, bamboo shoots, and water chestnuts. Stir-fry over medium-high heat for 3 minutes. Reduce heat to medium, cover wok, and cook for 5 to 6 minutes, stirring occasionally. Add chicken and mix together.
4. In a small bowl, combine water, cornstarch, soy sauce, bouillon granules, sugar, and garlic powder. Add mixture to wok and stir until sauce has thickened.
5. On each of five individual serving plates, spoon one-fifth of the mixture over ½ cup rice. Serve immediately.

Serves 5
Approximately 4 grams fat per serving

SUGGESTED ACCOMPANIMENTS (see Index)
Green salad with Sweet Honey Mustard Dressing
Butter-Glazed Carrots
Dropped Strawberries

CHEESY CORN AND "HAM" CHOWDER

A wholesome country-flavored soup made with fresh vegetables, turkey ham, and cheese.

1 cup frozen corn kernels, thawed
¾ cup chopped celery
3 ounces turkey ham, chopped
  (¾ cup)
½ cup chopped green bell pepper
½ cup chopped yellow onion
3⅓ cups skim milk
½ cup water
2 tablespoons flour
2 teaspoons chicken bouillon
  granules
½ cup grated reduced-fat sharp
  cheddar cheese
⅔ cup seeded chopped tomato
1–2 dashes hot sauce
Salt and pepper to taste

1. Combine corn, celery, turkey ham, green bell pepper, onion, 3 cups of the skim milk, and water in a large pot.

2. In a small bowl, mix together flour, bouillon granules, and remaining ⅓ cup skim milk. Add to ingredients in pot and stir.

3. Over medium-high heat, bring the mixture to a boil. Reduce heat and simmer, uncovered, for 45 minutes or until vegetables are tender, stirring occasionally.

4. Remove pot from heat. Add cheese, tomato, hot sauce, salt, and pepper to soup. Stir until cheese has melted and serve immediately.

Serves 4
Approximately 4.7 grams fat per serving

SUGGESTED ACCOMPANIMENTS (see Index)

Old-Fashioned Coleslaw
Oven-Fried Mushrooms and Zucchini
My Willie's Apples

"HAM" AND POTATO CASSEROLE IN CHEESE SAUCE

This is a hearty dish, sure to satisfy your appetite for a creamy, rich main course. Be sure to use boiled potatoes as called for because the precooked potatoes will absorb the flavors of the other ingredients beautifully; raw potatoes will simply water down the casserole.

Low-calorie cooking spray
5 ounces turkey ham, sliced thin
    and cut into bite-sized pieces
    (1¼ cups)
⅔ cup sliced yellow onion
½ medium-sized green bell
    pepper, sliced
4 medium-sized potatoes
    (1¼ pounds total), peeled if
    desired and boiled until tender
1 cup skim milk
1½ teaspoons cornstarch
½ cup grated reduced-fat cheddar
    cheese
Dash cayenne pepper
Salt and pepper to taste
Paprika

1. Preheat oven to 300°F.
2. Coat a large skillet with low-calorie cooking spray. Heat skillet. Add turkey ham, onion, and bell pepper and sauté over medium-high heat until onions begin to brown (3 to 5 minutes).
3. Slice boiled potatoes. Arrange half of the potatoes in the bottom of a 7″ × 11″ casserole dish. Top potatoes with turkey ham, onion, and bell pepper mixture. Place remaining half of potatoes on top.
4. In a small saucepan, combine skim milk and cornstarch. Over medium-high heat, heat mixture to a boil, stirring constantly. Boil for 1 minute. Remove saucepan from heat. Add cheese, cayenne pepper, and salt and pepper to taste. Stir until cheese has melted and pour sauce over potatoes.
5. Lightly sprinkle paprika over top of casserole. Bake, uncovered, for 30 minutes.

Serves 4
Approximately 4.8 grams fat per serving

SUGGESTED ACCOMPANIMENTS (see Index)

A Family Reunion Salad
Country Beans
Ambrosia

LEMON CHICKEN WITH ALMONDS

Lightly battered chicken in a rich, lemony sauce, topped with toasted almonds.

4 4-ounce skinless, boneless
chicken breast halves
3 tablespoons flour
3 tablespoons low-calorie
margarine
1 tablespoon olive oil
1 medium-sized garlic clove,
minced
½ cup chopped scallion
1 cup water
1 teaspoon chicken bouillon
granules
1 tablespoon fresh lemon juice
½ teaspoon grated lemon zest
2 tablespoons chopped fresh
parsley
2 tablespoons sliced almonds,
toasted (see notes)

1. Preheat oven to 350°F.
2. Flatten each piece of chicken to a ¼-inch thickness (see notes). Using a sifter, coat each piece with flour.
3. Heat 2 tablespoons of the margarine, the olive oil, and garlic in a nonstick skillet. Add chicken and cook over medium-high heat for 2 to 3 minutes on each side or until golden brown. Transfer chicken to a baking dish and place in oven. Bake for 8 to 10 minutes or until chicken is thoroughly cooked.
4. While chicken is baking, add remaining tablespoon margarine and scallion to skillet and sauté over medium heat until scallion is slightly translucent (2 to 3 minutes). Add water, bouillon granules, lemon juice, and lemon zest. Bring mixture to a boil, scraping the sides of the skillet occasionally. Simmer until sauce has thickened slightly (about 5 minutes).
5. Pour sauce over chicken pieces. Garnish with parsley and almonds.

Serves 4
Approximately 12.8 grams fat per serving

Notes: To toast almonds, simply cook them under the broiler until the pieces begin to brown, watching carefully to prevent burning.

To flatten chicken breasts, put one breast half between two sheets of wax paper and pound with a meat mallet, rolling pin, or heavy-bottomed pan, being careful not to tear chicken.

Variation: Substitute 2 tablespoons capers for the almonds.

SUGGESTED ACCOMPANIMENTS (see Index)

Green salad with Zesty Lemon Vinaigrette
Baked Cloved Onions
Strawberries in Vanilla Cream

SICILIAN CHICKEN SOUP

A delicious chicken soup with sweet onions and peppers, tomatoes, and noodles.

1¼ pounds skinless chicken breasts
1 quart water
Salt and pepper to taste
¼ teaspoon garlic powder
½ teaspoon paprika
1 medium-sized yellow onion,
    chopped
1 medium-sized green bell pepper,
    chopped
⅓ cup "lite" catsup
1 cup cooked egg noodles

1. Place chicken, water, salt and pepper to taste, garlic powder, and paprika in a Dutch oven or soup pot. Cover tightly and simmer for 50 minutes.
2. Add onion, bell pepper, and catsup. Cover and cook for 30 minutes more.
3. Remove chicken meat from bones, discarding bones. Cut meat into bite-sized pieces and return to pot.
4. Add noodles and cook over low heat for 10 minutes. Serve.

Serves 4
Approximately 3 grams fat per serving

SUGGESTED ACCOMPANIMENTS (see Index)

Green salad with Sweet Basil Vinaigrette
Steamed Broccoli with freshly squeezed lemon juice
My Willie's Apples

CHICKEN AND WILD RICE CASSEROLE

Succulent layers of chicken, wild rice, onion, and other delectable ingredients baked in a rich cream sauce.

2½ cups cooked packaged wild-and-white-rice blend (no margarine added during cooking)
1⅓ cups chopped cooked chicken breast meat
½ cup chopped yellow onion
½ cup drained sliced water chestnuts
1 2-ounce jar chopped pimiento, undrained
1⅓ cups cooked green beans
⅔ cup undiluted condensed cream of chicken soup
½ cup buttermilk
Salt and pepper to taste
Paprika

1. Preheat oven to 350°F.

2. In a 7″ × 11″ casserole dish, layer rice, chicken, onion, water chestnuts, pimiento, and green beans.

3. In a small bowl, combine soup and buttermilk. Blend well and spoon mixture over casserole. Sprinkle with salt, pepper, and paprika.

4. Bake, uncovered, for 30 to 35 minutes or until thoroughly heated. Let stand for 10 minutes before serving.

Serves 4
Approximately 4 grams fat per serving

SUGGESTED ACCOMPANIMENTS (see Index)

Hot Curried Fruit
Asparagus with Delicate Mustard Sauce
Chocolate Meringue Puffs

THAI-STYLE HOT CURRIED CHICKEN

Stir-fried chicken, green bell pepper, and onions with a distinctively delicious hot curry and brown sugar seasoning.

¼ cup plus 1 teaspoon "lite" soy sauce

2½ teaspoons cornstarch

¾ pound skinless, boneless chicken breasts, cut into bite-sized pieces

Low-calorie cooking spray

2 teaspoons vegetable oil

¾ cup sliced yellow onion

1½ medium-sized green bell peppers, sliced

1 8-ounce can bamboo shoots, thoroughly drained

½ teaspoon garlic powder

½ teaspoon hot red pepper flakes

Dash black pepper

⅓ cup water

1 tablespoon curry powder

1 tablespoon plus 1 teaspoon dark brown sugar (not packed)

2 cups hot cooked white rice (no margarine added during cooking)

1. In a shallow pan, combine 3 tablespoons of the soy sauce with 1½ teaspoons of the cornstarch. Add chicken and marinate for 30 minutes.

2. Coat a wok with low-calorie cooking spray. Add 1 teaspoon of the oil and heat. Add chicken and marinade. Cook over high heat until done (about 3 minutes), stirring frequently. Remove chicken from wok and set aside.

3. Add remaining teaspoon oil to wok. Heat oil to medium-high and add onion, bell pepper, and bamboo shoots. Stir-fry until onion is slightly translucent (about 2 minutes). Add chicken, garlic powder, red pepper flakes, and black pepper. Heat thoroughly.

4. Toss well. Remove from heat, cover and let stand 3 minutes until vegetables are tender but crisp.

5. In a small bowl, combine water, remaining soy sauce, and remaining cornstarch. Pour into wok. Heat for 1 minute, stirring constantly. Add curry powder and stir well. Add brown sugar and stir again.

6. On four individual serving plates, top ½ cup rice with one-quarter of the chicken mixture. Serve immediately.

Serves 4
Approximately 5.1 grams fat per serving

SUGGESTED ACCOMPANIMENTS (see Index)

Mandarin Salad with Almonds
Brown-Buttered Asparagus
Baked Pears in Orange-Raisin Sauce

MANDARIN CHICKEN SALAD

This delightful combination of chicken, oranges, and celery marinated in a sweet curry cream is a refreshing dish for hot summer nights.

1¼ pounds skinless chicken breast
    halves
Salt and pepper to taste
½ teaspoon poultry seasoning
1 cup well-drained canned
    mandarin oranges
¾ cup halved white seedless grapes
½ cup chopped celery
⅓ cup plain nonfat yogurt
¼ cup low-calorie mayonnaise
1 tablespoon plus 2 teaspoons
    sugar
1½ teaspoons curry powder
¼ teaspoon salt
⅛ teaspoon pepper

1. Put a small amount of water in a large pot and place a vegetable steamer in the pot. Add chicken and sprinkle with salt and pepper to taste and poultry seasoning. Cover pot and steam chicken over medium-high heat until thoroughly cooked (about 25 minutes). Remove chicken from pot and remove meat from bones, discarding bones. Chop meat into bite-sized pieces and place in a large salad bowl. Chill.

2. In a small mixing bowl, combine oranges, grapes, celery, yogurt, mayonnaise, sugar, curry powder, ¼ teaspoon salt, and ⅛ teaspoon pepper. Mix in with cooled chicken. Cover bowl and refrigerate for at least 2 hours.

Serves 4
Approximately 9.3 grams fat per serving

SUGGESTED ACCOMPANIMENTS (see Index)

Gingered Fruit Kabobs
Butter-Glazed Carrots
Coconut Meringues with Pineapple Filling

HEARTY COUNTRY CHICKEN SOUP

This is a favorite for a cold, blustery night. It's a wonderfully flavored cream soup with a bounty of garden vegetables.

5 cups chicken broth (homemade or canned)
1 cup water
⅓ cup uncooked white rice
2 medium-sized carrots, sliced diagonally
2 medium-sized stalks celery, sliced diagonally
2 small zucchini, diced
1⅓ cups skim milk
¼ cup flour
1⅓ cups diced cooked chicken breast meat
¼ cup chopped scallion
1 tablespoon plus 1 teaspoon chicken bouillon granules
Salt and pepper to taste
1 tablespoon chopped fresh parsley

1. In a large soup pot, bring broth to a full boil. Add rice and carrots. Cover pot and simmer for 10 minutes. Add celery and zucchini and simmer for 10 minutes more.
2. In a saucepan, combine skim milk and flour. Over medium heat, stir constantly with a whisk, until sauce has thickened slightly. Remove 1 cup broth from soup mixture and add to sauce. Bring to a boil.
3. Add sauce, chicken, scallion, bouillon granules, and 1 cup of water to soup pot. Heat thoroughly, adding salt and pepper to taste. Remove from heat. Add parsley and serve.

Serves 4
Approximately 2.3 grams fat per serving

SUGGESTED ACCOMPANIMENTS (see Index)

Old-Fashioned Coleslaw
Oven-Fried Okra
Baked Apples with Whipped Cream

CHICKEN IN A POT

This richly flavored dish offers generous portions—it's terrific on days when you're especially hungry.

Low-calorie cooking spray
4 6-ounce skinless chicken breast
  halves
1¼ cups homemade or canned
  chicken broth
¾ cup water
½ teaspoon salt
¼ teaspoon paprika
¼ teaspoon pepper
1 bay leaf
4 medium-sized cabbage wedges
1½ cups diagonally sliced celery
1 medium-sized yellow onion, cut
  into 8 uniformly sized wedges
1 cup diagonally sliced carrots
1 cup sliced green bell pepper
¼ cup chopped fresh parsley

1. Coat a soup pot with low-calorie cooking spray. Heat pot. Add chicken and cook over medium-high heat for about 3 minutes on each side, until browned. Add broth, water, salt, paprika, pepper, and bay leaf. Bring to a boil, reduce heat, cover pot, and simmer for 40 minutes.

2. Add cabbage, celery, onion, carrots, bell pepper, and parsley. Simmer, covered, for 20 minutes more. Remove bay leaf and serve.

Serves 4
Approximately 4.7 grams fat per serving

SUGGESTED ACCOMPANIMENTS (see Index)

Green salad with Thousand Island Dressing
Country Beans
Baked Pears in Orange-Raisin Sauce

ROASTED CHICKEN BREASTS

Simply seasoned with herbs and fresh parsley, this main course is perfect for accompanying more elegant side dishes.

2 tablespoons finely chopped fresh parsley
½ teaspoon poultry seasoning
½ teaspoon paprika
¼ teaspoon black pepper
¼ teaspoon salt
⅛ teaspoon garlic powder
4 8-ounce skinless chicken breast halves

1. Preheat oven to 350°F.
2. In a mixing bowl, combine parsley, poultry seasoning, paprika, pepper, salt, and garlic powder. Place chicken on the rack of a broiling pan and sprinkle seasoning mixture evenly over each piece. Bake for 35 to 40 minutes and serve.

Serves 4
Approximately 4.5 grams fat per serving

SUGGESTED ACCOMPANIMENTS (see Index)

The Stacked Salad
Mother's Cabbage
Rhubarb-Pineapple Compote

SMOTHERED CHICKEN

Tender roasted chicken in a succulent brown gravy.

4 8-ounce skinless chicken breast
  halves
Pepper to taste
¼ teaspoon garlic powder
¼ teaspoon paprika
2 tablespoons plus 1½ teaspoons
  flour
1½ cups water
1 tablespoon chicken bouillon
  granules

1. Preheat broiler.
2. Place chicken on a broiling pan. Sprinkle with pepper, garlic powder, and paprika. Broil, about 5 inches from the heat source, for 8 to 10 minutes or until chicken is thoroughly cooked.
3. While chicken is cooking, place flour in a dry iron skillet over medium-high heat. Stir constantly, until flour is a golden brown. (Be careful not to burn or scorch it.)
4. Add water and bouillon granules to flour. Stir until granules have dissolved and gravy is thoroughly blended. Remove chicken from oven and place in skillet. Cover and simmer for 20 minutes, stirring occasionally.
5. Arrange chicken on a serving platter and spoon sauce evenly over each piece.

Serves 4
Approximately 5.1 grams fat per serving

SUGGESTED ACCOMPANIMENTS (see Index)

Old-Fashioned Coleslaw
Country Turnips
Five-Fruit Cup

SIMKO'S CACCIATORE

This Hungarian version of cacciatore is my father's specialty—chicken simmered in a seasoned onion, pepper, and tomato sauce, served over pasta.

4 5-ounce skinless chicken breast
   halves
1⅓ cups water
Salt and pepper to taste
¼ teaspoon garlic powder
½ teaspoon paprika
1 medium-sized yellow onion,
   sliced thick
1 large green bell pepper, sliced
   thick
3 tablespoons "lite" catsup
2 cups hot cooked spaghetti

1. Place chicken in a deep skillet. Add water, then sprinkle chicken with salt and pepper, garlic powder, and paprika. Bring mixture to a boil, then cover skillet and reduce heat. Simmer for 35 minutes.

2. Add onion, pepper, and catsup. Cover and let simmer for 35 to 40 minutes more.

3. On each of four individual serving plates, place ½ cup spaghetti. Top each with one piece of chicken and spoon sauce evenly over each serving.

Serves 4
Approximately 3.6 grams fat per serving

SUGGESTED ACCOMPANIMENTS (see Index)

Green salad with Italian's Italian
Country Beans
Baked Apples with Whipped Cream

SOUTHERN OVEN-FRIED CHICKEN

A most flavorful fried chicken. I like to prepare this dish for my children's school lunches.

4 6½-ounce skinless chicken breast
   halves
½ cup buttermilk
½ cup flour
Low-calorie cooking spray
Salt and pepper to taste
Cajun seasoning to taste

1. Preheat oven to 350°F.
2. Place chicken in a shallow baking dish. Pour buttermilk over chicken and refrigerate for at least 20 minutes.
3. Using a sifter, coat each chicken piece with flour and place meat side down on a nonstick cookie sheet coated with low-calorie cooking spray. Sprinkle with salt, pepper, and Cajun seasoning to taste.
4. Bake for 30 minutes. Turn chicken pieces over and sprinkle lightly with salt, pepper, and Cajun seasoning. Bake for 30 to 40 minutes more or until chicken is thoroughly cooked.

Serves 4
Approximately 4.4 grams fat per serving

SUGGESTED ACCOMPANIMENTS (see Index)

Summer's Cucumbers
Summer Squash Casserole
Chocolate-Drizzled Fruit Kabobs

LEMON CURRY CHICKEN WITH BROCCOLI AND CHEESE

This dish is easy to make ahead of time. Simply prepare it as directed, then refrigerate overnight. Reheat it for 30 minutes, and you have dinner.

2 10-ounce packages frozen broccoli spears, lightly steamed

2 cups chopped cooked chicken breast meat

1 cup undiluted condensed cream of chicken soup

1 cup plain nonfat yogurt

1 tablespoon fresh lemon juice

½ teaspoon curry powder

½ cup grated reduced-fat cheddar cheese

1 slice "diet" bread, toasted and grated

1. Preheat oven to 350°F.
2. Place broccoli in a 7″ × 11″ casserole dish. Arrange chicken pieces on top of broccoli.
3. In a separate bowl, combine soup, yogurt, lemon juice, and curry. Spoon mixture over chicken. Sprinkle with cheese, then top with bread crumbs. Bake, uncovered, for 20 minutes or until casserole is thoroughly heated and cheese is bubbly.

Serves 4
Approximately 7.1 grams fat per serving

SUGGESTED ACCOMPANIMENTS (see Index)

Gingered Fruit Kabobs
A Finely Broiled Tomato
Pineapple Supreme

SPECIAL-OCCASION CHICKEN

This tender chicken and mushrooms in a luscious cream sauce is a wonderful dish to serve when entertaining.

Low-calorie cooking spray
4 7-ounce skinless chicken breast
   halves
½ pound fresh mushrooms, sliced
¼ cup chopped scallion
1 tablespoon butter or margarine
2 tablespoons flour
½ cup plain nonfat yogurt
¼ cup water
2 tablespoons cooking sherry
1 teaspoon chicken bouillon
   granules
½ teaspoon salt
¼ teaspoon ground nutmeg

1. Preheat oven to 350°F.
2. Coat a skillet with low-calorie cooking spray. Heat skillet. Add chicken and cook over medium-high heat until chicken is browned (2 to 3 minutes). Transfer chicken to a baking dish. Place mushrooms in skillet and sauté over medium-high heat for 3 to 4 minutes. Spoon mushrooms over chicken. Top with scallion and set aside.
3. Place butter or margarine in the skillet. Melt over medium heat and remove skillet from heat. Add flour and blend well. Add yogurt, water, sherry, bouillon granules, salt, and nutmeg. Stir well and pour sauce over chicken.
4. Bake for 25 to 30 minutes or until chicken is thoroughly cooked. (Note: After 15 minutes of cooking, you may want to baste chicken with sauce.)

Serves 4
Approximately 6.9 grams fat per serving

SUGGESTED ACCOMPANIMENTS (see Index)

Green salad with Simply Blue
Creamed Spinach
Cherries in Champagne

CHICKEN MONTEREY

Cheese-stuffed chicken, delicately herbed, battered, and browned.

4 4-ounce skinless, boneless
   chicken breast halves
1 medium-sized lemon
Salt and pepper to taste
Paprika to taste
2 ounces reduced-fat Monterey
   Jack cheese, cut into 4 equal
   slices
1 medium-sized egg
2 teaspoons freshly grated Romano
   cheese
½ teaspoon dried tarragon leaves
½ teaspoon chicken bouillon
   granules
2 tablespoons flour
1 tablespoon plus 2 teaspoons
   olive oil

1. Preheat oven to 375°F.
2. Place chicken on a plate and squeeze lemon juice evenly over each piece. Sprinkle with salt, pepper, and paprika.
3. Cut a pocket in the thickest side of each chicken piece just large enough in length to hold one cheese slice. Place one slice cheese in each pocket and pinch edges of pocket closed.
4. In a small bowl, combine egg, Romano cheese, tarragon, and bouillon granules. Beat well. Using a sifter, coat each chicken piece with flour and dip into egg mixture.
5. Place oil in a skillet and heat over medium-high heat. Add chicken and cook for 2 to 3 minutes on each side, until browned. Transfer chicken to a baking dish and bake, uncovered, for 8 to 10 minutes or until chicken is thoroughly cooked.

Serves 4
Approximately 12.6 grams fat per serving

SUGGESTED ACCOMPANIMENTS (see Index)

Green salad with Italian's Italian
Broiled Tomatoes Dijon
Tropical Citrus Freeze

INDIVIDUAL POTATO PUFFS

Fluffy whipped potatoes combined with turkey ham, cheese, onion, and fresh parsley, with just a touch of cayenne pepper.

3 medium-sized potatoes
   (1½ pounds total), peeled and
   boiled until tender
1¼ cups skim milk
1 tablespoon plus 1 teaspoon
   chopped fresh parsley
Dash cayenne pepper
Salt and pepper to taste
Paprika to taste
Low-calorie cooking spray
¼ pound turkey ham, sliced thin
3 tablespoons finely chopped
   yellow onion
⅔ cup grated reduced-fat cheddar
   cheese

1. Preheat oven to 350°F.
2. In a mixing bowl, mash or whip potatoes with milk, parsley, cayenne pepper, salt, pepper, and paprika.
3. Coat a nonstick skillet with low-calorie cooking spray. Heat skillet. Add turkey ham and brown over medium-high heat for 2 to 3 minutes.
4. Place the potatoes in four individual casserole dishes. Top with turkey ham and onion. Sprinkle cheese evenly over each and bake for 20 minutes or until casseroles are thoroughly heated.

Serves 4
Approximately 5.4 grams fat per serving

SUGGESTED ACCOMPANIMENTS (see Index)

Spicy Peaches
Sautéed Cabbage
Banana Cream Supreme

SCALLOPED "HAM" AND POTATO CASSEROLE

This dish has a very homey, mild flavor that appeals to children or anyone in need of some "comfort food."

1¼ cups skim milk
¾ cup evaporated skim milk
3 tablespoons flour
¼ teaspoon salt
¼ teaspoon pepper
4 small potatoes (1¼ pounds total), peeled, if desired, diced and boiled
¼ pound turkey ham, sliced thin
¼ cup finely chopped yellow onion

1. Preheat oven to 350°F.
2. In a saucepan, combine skim milk, evaporated skim milk, flour, salt, and pepper. Over medium-high heat, stir constantly, until sauce has thickened.
3. Place half of the potatoes on the bottom of a 9-inch square baking dish. Next add half of the turkey ham, then half of the onions, then half of the sauce. Repeat each layer and bake, uncovered, for 55 to 60 minutes.

Serves 4
Approximately 2.7 grams fat per serving

SUGGESTED ACCOMPANIMENTS (see Index)

Tangy Cranberry Fiesta Salad
Country Turnips
Five-Fruit Cup

JALAPEÑO, BEAN, AND "HAM" SOUP WITH CHEESE

A hot and hearty soup capped with cheddar cheese and onion.

½ cup dried black beans
⅓ cup dried red kidney beans
6 cups water
3 ounces turkey ham, chopped
   (¾ cup)
1 cup chopped celery
¾ cup chopped yellow onion
1 medium-sized clove garlic,
   minced
1 16-ounce can tomatoes,
   undrained
2 fresh jalapeño peppers, seeded
   and chopped fine
2 tablespoons chili powder
1 teaspoon ground cumin
½ teaspoon dried oregano leaves
1 teaspoon salt
Pepper to taste
½ cup grated reduced-fat cheddar
   cheese
¼ cup chopped scallion

1. Soak black and kidney beans overnight. Drain.

2. In a large soup pot, combine beans, water, and all other ingredients except cheese and scallion. Cover pot and bring mixture to a boil. Reduce heat and simmer for 2 to 2½ hours.

3. Divide soup evenly among four individual soup bowls. Top each bowl with 2 tablespoons cheese and 1 tablespoon scallion. Serve immediately.

Serves 4
Approximately 4.5 grams fat per serving

SUGGESTED ACCOMPANIMENTS (see Index)

Green salad with Creamy Avocado Dressing
Oven-Fried Okra
Tropical Lemon Cream Squares

APRICOT "HAM" STEAK

This dish is very easy to prepare, yet it's quite festive—baked turkey ham seasoned with brown sugar, apricots, and cloves.

4 ¼-pound slices turkey ham
¼ cup dark brown sugar (not packed)
16 cloves
1 8-ounce can apricot halves in their own juice, drained

1. Preheat oven to 325°F.
2. Place turkey ham in one layer in an 8″ × 12″ baking dish. Stud each slice with four cloves. Divide apricot halves among the turkey ham slices. Sprinkle with brown sugar. Bake for 30 minutes, basting occasionally.

Serves 4
Approximately 5.6 grams fat per serving

SUGGESTED ACCOMPANIMENTS (see Index)

Waldorf Salad
Broccoli with Mild Lemon Curry Sauce
Chocolate Dreams

CHICKEN SUPREME

I often make this when I'm running short of time but still want a flavorful main course.

4 8-ounce skinless chicken breasts
1 cup plain nonfat yogurt
2 tablespoons dried French onion soup mix
Paprika

1. Preheat oven to 350°F.
2. Place chicken in one layer in a casserole dish. In a separate bowl, combine yogurt and soup mix. Blend well and spoon evenly over chicken. Sprinkle with paprika and bake, uncovered, for 45 minutes.

Serves 4
Approximately 4.8 grams fat per serving

SUGGESTED ACCOMPANIMENTS (see Index)

Lemon-Limed Tomatoes
Country Beans
Chocolate Crumb "Crème de Menthe"

SKEWERED CHICKEN AND BEEF ORIENTAL

Succulent meats marinated in soy sauce and brown sugar and grilled with onions, sweet peppers, and pineapple.

¼ cup "lite" soy sauce
¼ cup dark brown sugar (not packed)
½ teaspoon ground ginger
¼ teaspoon garlic powder
10 ounces skinless, boneless chicken breast, cut into 8 uniformly sized pieces
5 ounces boneless lean round steak, cut into 4 uniformly sized pieces
Low-calorie cooking spray
1 medium-sized yellow onion, cut into 8 uniformly sized wedges
1 cup pineapple chunks (if canned, in their own juice, drained)
1 medium-sized red bell pepper, cut into 1-inch chunks

1. Mix together soy sauce, brown sugar, ginger, and garlic powder. Pour over chicken and beef and refrigerate in an airtight container for 8 hours.
2. Preheat the broiler. Drain meat, reserving marinade.
3. Liberally coat four skewers with low-calorie cooking spray. On each skewer, thread two pieces chicken, one piece steak, two onion wedges, ¼ cup pineapple chunks, and one-quarter of the bell pepper chunks, alternating ingredients.
4. Broil skewers, 2–3 inches from the heat source, for 3 to 5 minutes, basting occasionally with reserved marinade.

Serves 4
Approximately 3 grams fat per serving

SUGGESTED ACCOMPANIMENTS (see Index)

From a Corner of Chinatown
Butter-Glazed Carrots
Gingered Fruit in Plum Wine

MAIN COURSES
✤ SEAFOOD ✤

CRAB QUICHE WITH WINE

An elegant quiche filled with Swiss cheese, crabmeat, and zesty scallions.

⅓ cup low-calorie mayonnaise
1 tablespoon plus 1 teaspoon flour
2 medium-sized eggs, beaten
⅓ cup evaporated skim milk
⅓ cup dry white wine, cooked
   down to 3 tablespoons and
   cooled
1 cup cooked crabmeat
¾ cup grated reduced-fat Swiss
   cheese
¼ cup chopped scallion

1. Preheat oven to 350°F.
2. In a small bowl, combine mayonnaise and flour. Set aside.
3. Place eggs in a separate bowl. While beating eggs, add evaporated skim milk and wine. Mix thoroughly with mayonnaise mixture, then stir in crab, cheese, and scallion.
4. Spoon mixture into a 9-inch pie pan. Bake for 25 to 30 minutes or until quiche is firm in the center.

Serves 4
Approximately 15.1 grams fat per serving

SUGGESTED ACCOMPANIMENTS (see Index)

Gingered Fruit Kabobs
A Finely Broiled Tomato
Tropical Citrus Freeze

THE BAY'S BEST SEAFOOD GUMBO

Piping hot shrimp, crab, and vegetables packed with flavor and served over rice.

1½ teaspoons butter or margarine
1½ teaspoons vegetable shortening
1 tablespoon flour
⅔ cup finely chopped yellow
   onion
1 cup finely chopped celery
½ medium-sized green bell
   pepper, chopped fine
1 clove garlic, minced
1 16-ounce can tomatoes,
   undrained
½ pound fresh okra, sliced
6 cups water
1 cup cooked crabmeat
½ cup peeled and deveined shrimp
1 tablespoon Worcestershire sauce
1 small bay leaf
1 teaspoon salt
Black and cayenne pepper to taste
Hot sauce to taste
2 cups hot cooked white rice (no
   margarine added during
   cooking)

1. In a large Dutch oven (iron, if possible), combine butter or margarine, shortening, and flour over medium heat. Stir constantly, until mixture turns a dark brown (5 to 6 minutes). Stir in onions, celery, green bell pepper, and garlic. Simmer, uncovered, for 5 minutes, stirring frequently.

2. Add tomatoes and okra and simmer until okra is tender yet still crisp (about 15 minutes). Add water, crabmeat, shrimp, Worcestershire sauce, bay leaf, salt, black and cayenne pepper, and hot sauce. Cover pot and simmer for 2 hours.

3. Remove bay leaf. Place ½ cup rice in each of four individual soup bowls. Top with one-quarter of the gumbo and serve.

Serves 4
Approximately 4 grams fat per serving

Note: The flavor of the gumbo improves if refrigerated overnight and reheated. The gumbo (but not the rice) also freezes well.

SUGGESTED ACCOMPANIMENTS (see Index)

Green salad with Italian's Italian
Country Beans
Pineapple Supreme

CRAB GENEVA

This elegant dish—spinach smothered in a succulent Swiss cheese and crab cream sauce topped with bread crumbs—is easy to prepare.

2 10-ounce packages frozen chopped spinach, cooked and squeezed dry
⅛ teaspoon garlic powder
1 tablespoon grated yellow onion
2 tablespoons flour
1½ cups skim milk
¼ teaspoon salt
½ cup grated reduced-fat Swiss cheese
½ cup evaporated skim milk
1 teaspoon fresh lemon juice
¼ teaspoon cayenne pepper
⅛ teaspoon ground nutmeg
1 pound cooked crabmeat
1 slice "diet" bread, toasted and grated

1. Preheat the broiler.
2. Place spinach in a 2-quart casserole dish. Sprinkle with garlic powder and onion.
3. In a small jar, place flour plus ¼ cup of the skim milk. Shake until mixture is thoroughly blended. Pour into a saucepan and add the remaining 1¼ cups skim milk and the salt over medium heat. Stir constantly, until mixture has thickened. Simmer for 1 minute and add cheese, evaporated skim milk, lemon juice, cayenne pepper, and nutmeg. Stir until cheese has melted.
4. Remove pan from heat and carefully fold crabmeat into the mixture. Pour over spinach and sprinkle with bread crumbs. Broil, 5 inches from the heat source, for 2 to 3 minutes or until bread crumbs have browned.

Serves 4
Approximately 4.1 grams fat per serving

SUGGESTED ACCOMPANIMENTS (see Index)

Green salad with Sweet Basil Vinaigrette
Butter-Glazed Carrots
Frozen Sugar-Coated Grapes

CRAB CASSEROLE WITH CHEESE

Crab, mushrooms, onion, and celery baked in a luscious cheese sauce.

Low-calorie cooking spray
2 cups sliced fresh mushrooms
1 teaspoon vegetable oil
⅔ cup finely chopped yellow
   onion
1 medium-sized stalk celery,
   chopped fine
2 tablespoons plus 2 teaspoons
   flour
1½ cups skim milk
2 medium-sized eggs
¾ teaspoon salt
½ teaspoon cayenne pepper
⅛ teaspoon black pepper
1¼ cups cooked crabmeat
1 cup grated reduced-fat sharp
   cheddar cheese

1. Preheat oven to 350°F.

2. Coat a nonstick skillet with low-calorie cooking spray. Heat skillet. Add mushrooms and sauté over medium-high heat for 3 to 4 minutes. Transfer mushrooms to another dish and set aside.

3. Add oil, onion, and celery to skillet. Sauté vegetables over medium heat until onion is slightly translucent (about 2 minutes).

4. Place flour and ½ cup of the skim milk in a small jar and shake until mixture is thoroughly blended. Transfer to a mixing bowl and add remaining cup of milk, eggs, salt, cayenne, and black pepper. Mix well and pour sauce over vegetables. Stir constantly over medium heat until mixture begins to thicken.

5. Carefully fold crabmeat and ½ cup of the cheese into mixture. Pour into a 2-quart baking dish and top with the remaining ½ cup of cheese. Bake for 15 to 20 minutes or until thoroughly heated. Serve immediately.

Serves 4
Approximately 9 grams fat per serving

SUGGESTED ACCOMPANIMENTS (see Index)

Lemon-Limed Tomatoes
Brown-Buttered Asparagus
Strawberry Sorbet

DEVILED CRAB AND SHRIMP SUPREME

Spicy sautéed seafood baked in a mixture of bread crumbs, vegetables, and Cajun seasonings.

1 tablespoon butter
Dash garlic salt
½ cup peeled cooked baby shrimp
⅛ teaspoon cayenne pepper
1¾ cups cooked crabmeat
¾ cup chopped celery
½ medium-sized green bell
    pepper, chopped
1 small yellow onion, chopped
1 cup skim milk
2 tablespoons flour
2 medium-sized egg whites, beaten
2½ teaspoons fresh lemon juice
2½ teaspoons prepared mustard
2½ teaspoons Worcestershire sauce
¼ teaspoon salt
⅛ teaspoon pepper
2 slices "diet" bread, toasted and
    grated
Low-calorie cooking spray
1 tablespoon butter, melted

1. Preheat the broiler.
2. In a saucepan, melt 1 tablespoon butter with garlic salt. Add shrimp and cayenne pepper and sauté for 3 minutes. Place shrimp in a bowl and add crabmeat.
3. To drippings in saucepan add celery, green bell pepper, onion, and ¾ cup of the skim milk. Place flour and remaining ¼ cup skim milk in a separate bowl. Blend thoroughly and add to saucepan. Over a medium-low heat, stir constantly, until mixture is well blended and sauce has thickened slightly. Pour mixture over shrimp and crabmeat.
4. Add egg whites, lemon juice, mustard, Worcestershire sauce, salt, pepper, and ½ of the bread crumbs to seafood mixture. Toss gently but thoroughly.
5. Coat four individual baking dishes with low-calorie cooking spray. Place one-quarter of the seafood mixture in each dish and top each with an equal amount of the remaining bread crumbs. Drizzle ¾ teaspoon melted butter evenly over each casserole. Broil, 2–3 inches from the heat source, for 2 to 3 minutes or until bread crumbs have browned. Serve immediately.

Serves 4
Approximately 8.3 grams fat per serving

SUGGESTED ACCOMPANIMENTS (see Index)

Lemon-Limed Tomatoes
Asparagus with Delicate Mustard Sauce
Tropical Citrus Freeze

HOT BUTTERED SHRIMP

Simple to prepare but sure to satisfy your taste for indulgence.

Low-calorie cooking spray
3 cups small peeled and deveined shrimp (1½ pounds)
1 stalk celery, cut into 2-inch pieces
1 medium-sized yellow onion, cut into eighths
¼ teaspoon cayenne pepper
Salt and pepper to taste
2 tablespoons fresh lemon juice
3 tablespoons plus 2 teaspoons butter or margarine, melted
Garnish: Lemon wedges

1. Coat a large nonstick skillet with low-calorie cooking spray. Heat skillet. Add shrimp, celery, onion, cayenne pepper, and salt and pepper to taste. Cook over medium-heat heat, stirring frequently, until shrimp become opaque (about 8 to 10 minutes).

2. Place shrimp in a decorative serving bowl. Discard celery and onions. Pour lemon juice and melted butter over shrimp. Toss well and garnish with lemon wedges. Serve immediately.

Serves 4
Approximately 11.4 grams fat per serving

SUGGESTED ACCOMPANIMENTS (see Index)

Garden and Pasta Salad
Baked Mélange
Blueberry and Lime Sorbet

SHRIMP SALAD WITH FRESH LEMON

A light, lemon-flavored toss of shrimp, celery, onion, and mayonnaise with just a touch of cayenne pepper.

4 cups small shrimp (boiled in crab boil until pink), peeled and deveined (2 pounds)
1 cup chopped celery
¼ cup chopped yellow onion
⅓ cup plus 1 teaspoon low-calorie mayonnaise
Juice of 1 medium-sized lemon
Salt and pepper to taste
⅛ teaspoon cayenne pepper
Garnish: Lettuce leaves and lemon wedges

1. Chop shrimp into small bite-sized pieces. Place in a mixing bowl and add celery and onion. Mix well and set aside.

2. In a separate bowl, combine mayonnaise, lemon juice, salt and pepper, and cayenne pepper. Blend well and add to shrimp mixture. Toss thoroughly and refrigerate for at least 2 hours.

3. Line four individual serving plates with lettuce leaves. Place ¾ cup salad on each plate and garnish with lemon wedges.

Serves 5
Approximately 5.4 grams fat per serving

SUGGESTED ACCOMPANIMENTS (see Index)

Gingered Fruit Kabobs
Lemon-Limed Tomatoes
Chocolate Dreams

CURRIED SHRIMP DELUXE

Shrimp and onions cooked in a delicately seasoned curry sauce, served over rice.

Low-calorie cooking spray
2¼ cups small peeled and deveined
   shrimp (1¼ pounds)
3 tablespoons minced yellow
   onion
2 teaspoons curry powder
1½ teaspoons sugar
¼ teaspoon ground nutmeg
¼ teaspoon paprika
Dash ground ginger
1 cup skim milk
2 tablespoons flour
½ teaspoon salt
1 tablespoon fresh lemon juice
Dash Worcestershire sauce
2 cups hot cooked white rice (no
   margarine added during
   cooking)
2 tablespoons chopped scallion

1. Coat a nonstick skillet with low-calorie cooking spray. Heat skillet. Add shrimp and yellow onion and sauté over medium-high heat for 2 minutes. Add curry powder, sugar, nutmeg, paprika, and ginger and heat for 3 to 5 minutes.

2. In a small jar, combine ¼ cup of the skim milk with flour and shake to blend thoroughly. Add mixture to shrimp along with the remaining ¾ cup milk. Stir and add salt, lemon juice, and Worcestershire sauce. Cook over medium-high heat until sauce has thickened (about 4 to 5 minutes). Remove from heat, cover, and let stand for 10 minutes.

3. Toss rice with scallion and place on a serving platter. Top with shrimp mixture and serve.

Serves 4
Approximately 1.1 grams fat per serving

Note: The flavor of this dish is greatly enhanced when it's refrigerated overnight.

SUGGESTED ACCOMPANIMENTS (see Index)

Mandarin Salad with Almonds
Peas and Water Chestnuts
Frozen Sugar-Coated Grapes

SHRIMP CREOLE

This festive dish is perfect for Mardi Gras celebrations or any other type of party.

2 teaspoons solid vegetable shortening
2 teaspoons flour
⅔ cup chopped celery
⅔ cup chopped yellow onion
½ large green bell pepper, chopped
2 cups small peeled and deveined shrimp (1 pound)
1 16-ounce can tomatoes, undrained
Juice of ½ medium-sized lemon
1 bay leaf
4–5 drops hot sauce
½ teaspoon Worcestershire sauce
⅛ teaspoon chili powder
¼ teaspoon paprika
Salt and pepper to taste
1 medium-sized clove garlic, minced
2 cups hot cooked white rice (no margarine added during cooking)

1. Melt shortening in a large iron Dutch oven over medium-high heat. Add flour and stir until mixture is a rich dark brown color (5 to 6 minutes). Add celery, onion, and bell pepper and cook until vegetables are tender yet still crisp (about 3 minutes).

2. Add shrimp, tomatoes, lemon juice, bay leaf, hot sauce, Worcestershire, chili powder, paprika, salt, pepper, and garlic. Bring to a boil. Reduce heat to medium-low, cover pot, and simmer for 25 to 30 minutes.

3. Place rice on a serving platter and spoon creole onto it.

Serves 4
Approximately 3.3 grams fat per serving

Note: The flavor of this dish is greatly enhanced when it is refrigerated overnight.

SUGGESTED ACCOMPANIMENTS (see Index)

Green salad with Creamy Garlic with Parmesan
Country Beans
Banana Cream Supreme

A SAILOR'S BARBECUE

Straight from the sea, this recipe is a delicious blend of shrimp, bacon, and water chestnuts in a sweet barbecue sauce.

Low-calorie cooking spray
2½ cups small peeled and deveined shrimp, with tails left on (2½ pounds)
4 bacon strips, cut into 8 pieces each
½ cup halved water chestnuts
⅔ cup "lite" catsup
⅓ cup water
2 tablespoons plus 2 teaspoons red wine vinegar
2 tablespoons plus 2 teaspoons dark brown sugar (not packed)
1 tablespoon plus 1 teaspoon Worcestershire sauce
1½ teaspoons chili powder
⅛ teaspoon salt
¼ teaspoon hot sauce
1 clove garlic, minced
⅓ teaspoon (1 packet) Equal

1. Preheat the broiler.
2. Coat eight skewers with low-calorie cooking spray. Thread an equal amount of the shrimp and four pieces bacon onto each of eight skewers, alternating ingredients.
3. In a saucepan, combine the remaining ingredients and bring to a boil. Allow mixture to boil until sauce has been reduced to ⅔ cup (5 to 6 minutes).
4. Coat a broiling pan with low-calorie cooking spray. Place skewers on the rack of the pan and baste with sauce. Broil, 2–3 inches away from the heat source, for 6 to 7 minutes, basting and turning skewers frequently, until bacon is thoroughly cooked.

Serves 4
Approximately 4.2 grams fat per serving

SUGGESTED ACCOMPANIMENTS (see Index)

Green salad with Thousand Island Dressing
All-American Oven Fries
Pineapple Supreme

SHRIMP AND MUSHROOMS ELEGANTE

First-class entertaining fare, this dish combines shrimp and mushrooms with soy sauce, lemon, and garlic and is served over rice.

1 cup small peeled and deveined shrimp (8 ounces)
1 pound fresh mushrooms, halved
½ teaspoon garlic powder
¼ cup "lite" soy sauce
¼ cup fresh lemon juice
1 tablespoon plus 1 teaspoon vegetable oil
2 tablespoons chopped fresh parsley
2 tablespoons water
2⅔ cups hot cooked white rice (no margarine or salt added during cooking)
3 tablespoons finely chopped scallion

1. Preheat the broiler.
2. Place shrimp and mushrooms in a shallow glass dish.
3. In a small bowl, combine garlic powder, soy sauce, lemon juice, vegetable oil, parsley, and water. Mix well and pour over shrimp and mushrooms. Marinate for 30 minutes.
4. Transfer shrimp, mushrooms, and marinade to a broiler pan and broil, about 5 inches from the heat source, for 2 to 3 minutes or until the shrimp curls. Stir and broil for 2 to 3 minutes more.
5. In a decorative serving bowl, toss together rice and scallion. Spoon shrimp mixture over rice and serve immediately.

Serves 4
Approximately 5.3 grams fat per serving

SUGGESTED ACCOMPANIMENTS (see Index)

Green salad with Creamy Dijon
Baked Cloved Onions
Meringues with Chocolate Mousse

ORIENTAL SHRIMP BALLS WITH SAUCES

Bite-sized morsels of shrimp, water chestnuts, and scallion served with two distinctly flavored sauces.

3 cups (about 1½ lbs.) small peeled and deveined shrimp, cooked (in crab boil if possible)
1 cup chopped water chestnuts, drained
1 teaspoon salt
¼ teaspoon garlic powder
2 teaspoons cornstarch
2 medium-sized eggs, beaten
¼ cup chopped scallion
Low-calorie cooking spray
2 tablespoons reduced-calorie grape jelly
2 tablespoons hot chili sauce
3 tablespoons Dijon mustard
2 teaspoons water
Dash hot sauce

1. Preheat the broiler.
2. Finely chop shrimp (if you have a food processor, use it). Place shrimp in bowl and add water chestnuts, salt, garlic powder, cornstarch, eggs, and scallion. Stir well and chill for 30 to 45 minutes.
3. Roll into 1-inch round balls. Coat a broiler pan with low-calorie cooking spray and place shrimp balls in pan. Broil, 2–3 inches from the heat source, for 5 to 6 minutes, turning frequently, until shrimp balls are browned.
4. While shrimp is broiling, mix together grape jelly and chili sauce. Heat in a saucepan over low heat.
5. In a separate bowl, mix together Dijon mustard, water, and hot sauce.
6. Place one-quarter of the shrimp balls on each of four individual serving plates. Spoon 1 tablespoon of each sauce onto each plate.

Serves 4
Approximately 4.7 grams fat per serving

SUGGESTED ACCOMPANIMENTS (see Index)

Green salad with Chinatown Soy
Fresh Broccoli and Ginger Oriental
Baked Pears in Orange-Raisin Sauce

FLOUNDER WITH GREEN BELL PEPPERS AND BORDER RICE

Delicately seasoned flounder, steamed with bell peppers and served with tomato-tossed rice.

Low-calorie cooking spray
4 4-ounce flounder fillets
1 medium-sized green bell pepper,
    cut into 12 rings
½ teaspoon garlic powder
½ teaspoon paprika
½ teaspoon Cajun seasoning
2⅔ cups hot cooked white rice,
    cooked with 1½ teaspoons beef
    bouillon granules (no margarine
    added during cooking)
½ teaspoon chili powder
1 cup chopped fresh tomato
3 tablespoons finely chopped
    yellow onion
Salt and pepper to taste
1 tablespoon plus 1 teaspoon
    butter

1. Preheat oven to 350°F.
2. Liberally coat one side of each of four 12-inch sheets of aluminum foil with low-calorie cooking spray. Place one piece fish on each sheet. Top each with 3 bell pepper rings. Sprinkle with garlic powder, paprika, and Cajun seasoning. Seal tightly. Place fish in oven and bake for 20 to 25 minutes.
3. While fish is cooking, toss together rice, chili powder, tomato, onion, salt, and pepper. Keep warm until ready to serve.
4. Just before serving, melt butter over high heat until bubbly and golden brown (about 3 minutes). Place an equal amount of rice mixture on each of four individual serving plates. Remove fish and bell peppers from foil and place one serving on each plate alongside or on top of rice. Drizzle 1 teaspoon butter over each serving of fish.

Serves 4
Approximately 3.5 grams fat per serving

SUGGESTED ACCOMPANIMENTS (see Index)

Green salad with Creamy Avocado Dressing
Cauliflower in Hot Cheese Sauce
Pineapple Supreme

BAKED FLOUNDER WITH CREAMY TARRAGON SAUCE

A mild, aromatic tarragon sauce gives this flounder, served with parsley-tossed rice, its tasty flavor.

Low-calorie cooking spray
4 4-ounce flounder fillets
⅓ cup low-calorie mayonnaise
2 tablespoons Dijon mustard
2 tablespoons skim milk
½ teaspoon dried tarragon leaves
2 cups hot cooked white rice (no margarine added during cooking)
2 teaspoons finely chopped fresh parsley

1. Preheat oven to 350°F.
2. Coat a nonstick cookie sheet with low-calorie cooking spray. Place fish on sheet.
3. In a small bowl, mix together mayonnaise, mustard, skim milk, and tarragon. Spoon an equal amount of mixture over each fillet. Bake, uncovered, for 20 minutes.
4. Toss together rice and parsley.
5. Just before serving, place ½ cup rice mixture on each of four individual serving plates. Place one piece fish alongside rice and serve.

Serves 4
Approximately 8.1 grams fat per serving

SUGGESTED ACCOMPANIMENTS (see Index)

Green salad with Zesty Lemon Vinaigrette
Peas and Water Chestnuts
Strawberry Sorbet

FLOUNDER AND BACON KABOBS WITH CREAMY BAKED POTATOES

Soy sauce gives these fillets a light Oriental flavor. Grilled with bacon and served with baked potatoes, the flounder dish makes a very satisfying meal.

4 4-ounce flounder fillets
4 bacon strips
¼ cup "lite" soy sauce
¾ cup low-fat (1 percent fat) cottage cheese
1 tablespoon grated yellow onion
Salt and pepper to taste
2 medium-sized potatoes (12 ounces total), baked and halved lengthwise
¼ cup chopped scallion

1. Preheat the broiler.
2. Slice each fillet into 1-inch-wide strips. Cut each bacon strip into 4 uniformly sized pieces. Place fish and bacon in a shallow glass dish. Cover with soy sauce and refrigerate for 30 minutes.
3. Using 4 skewers, thread equal amounts of fish and 4 pieces of bacon onto each skewer, alternating flounder and bacon pieces. Reserve marinade for basting.
4. Place skewers on a broiling pan. Broil, about 5 inches from the heat source, for 6 to 8 minutes, turning and basting with reserved marinade every 2 minutes or until bacon is thoroughly cooked.
5. While fish is cooking, place cottage cheese, onion, salt, and pepper in a blender. Blend until mixture is creamy.
6. Just before serving, spoon an equal amount of cottage cheese mixture over each potato half. Top with scallion and serve alongside fish and bacon skewers.

Serves 4
Approximately 4.2 grams fat per serving

SUGGESTED ACCOMPANIMENTS (see Index)

Green salad with Smooth and Creamy Blue
Baked Mélange
Chocolate Dreams

BROWN-BUTTERED FISH WITH TOASTED ALMONDS

Baked fillet of sole sprinkled with toasted almonds and drizzled with hot browned butter.

Low-calorie cooking spray
4 6-ounce sole fillets
2 teaspoons Worcestershire sauce
Salt and pepper to taste
1 teaspoon paprika
3 tablespoons plus 2 teaspoons butter
¼ cup almonds, toasted (see note)

1. Preheat oven to 350°F.
2. Coat a baking dish with low-calorie cooking spray. Place sole in one layer in the dish. Sprinkle each fillet with Worcestershire sauce, salt and pepper, and paprika. Bake uncovered for 15 to 20 minutes or until fish is cooked.
3. While fish is cooking, heat butter in a small saucepan, stirring constantly, until golden brown.
4. Remove fillets from baking dish, and place on a serving platter. Sprinkle toasted almonds over fillets. Drizzle an even amount of hot browned butter over each piece. Serve immediately.

Serves 4
Approximately 15.3 grams fat per serving

Note: To toast almonds, simply cook them under the broiler until they have browned, watching them carefully to prevent burning.

SUGGESTED ACCOMPANIMENTS (see Index)

Green salad with Simply Blue
Butter-Glazed Carrots
Cherries in Champagne

FISH CAKES DRIZZLED WITH BUTTER

Fish patties seasoned with Parmesan cheese, onion, parsley, and a dash of cayenne.

2 small potatoes (½ pound total), peeled
½ cup skim milk
1 pound skinned ocean perch or flounder fillets
4 slices "diet" bread, dried (*not* toasted) and grated
2 tablespoons chopped fresh parsley
2 tablespoons freshly grated Parmesan cheese
2 tablespoons finely chopped yellow onion
2 tablespoons minced celery
¼ teaspoon garlic powder
Salt and pepper to taste
⅛ teaspoon cayenne pepper
2 medium-sized egg whites, beaten
3 tablespoons plus 1 teaspoon butter

1. Preheat oven to 350°F.
2. Boil potatoes until tender. Drain. Add milk, mash potatoes, and set aside.
3. While potatoes are cooking, place fish in one layer in a shallow baking dish. Tightly cover dish with foil and bake for 20 to 25 minutes or until fish is cooked.
4. Flake fish and add to mashed potatoes. Mix in bread crumbs, parsley, cheese, onion, celery, garlic powder, salt, pepper, cayenne pepper, and egg whites. Blend well.
5. Form mixture into five uniformly sized patties (each patty should be ½ to ¾ inch thick). Place on a cookie sheet and bake for 20 minutes.
6. Melt butter in a small saucepan. Drizzle 1¼ teaspoons melted butter over each patty and serve immediately.

Serves 5
Approximately 9.7 grams fat per serving

SUGGESTED ACCOMPANIMENTS (see Index)

Old-Fashioned Coleslaw
Country Turnips
Strawberry-Crowned Lemon Chiffon

BAKED SNAPPER WITH HERBED BUTTER

Delicately flavored red snapper, topped with a luscious herbed butter and served with onion-tossed rice.

Low-calorie cooking spray
4 4-ounce red snapper fillets
Salt and pepper to taste
1 teaspoon paprika
¼ cup low-calorie margarine
1 teaspoon fresh lemon juice
½ teaspoon dried basil leaves
½ teaspoon dried parsley flakes
¼ teaspoon dried dill
Dash garlic powder
⅛ teaspoon salt
2 cups hot cooked white rice (no margarine added during cooking)
1 tablespoon finely chopped scallion
Garnish: Lemon wedges

1. Preheat oven to 350°F.
2. Coat a baking dish with low-calorie cooking spray. Place fillets in dish and sprinkle with salt, pepper, and paprika. Bake uncovered for 15 to 20 minutes or until cooked.
3. In a small bowl, combine margarine, lemon juice, basil, parsley, dill, garlic powder, and ⅛ teaspoon salt. Blend well.
4. Just before serving, toss together rice and scallion. Place ½ cup rice mixture on each of four individual serving plates. Place one fillet next to rice on each plate and top with 1 tablespoon herbed butter. Garnish with lemon wedges and serve.

Serves 4
Approximately 6.8 grams fat per serving

SUGGESTED ACCOMPANIMENTS (see Index)

Green salad with Creamy Avocado Dressing
Brown-Buttered Asparagus
Chocolate-Drizzled Fruit Kabobs

BAKED FLOUNDER WITH NEW POTATOES IN LEMON BUTTER

A light, easy-to-make dish that's sure to please even nondieters.

Low-calorie cooking spray
4 4-ounce flounder fillets
Salt and pepper to taste
1 teaspoon paprika
4 new potatoes (1 pound total)
3 tablespoons butter
1 teaspoon fresh lemon juice
Lemon pepper to taste
Dried parsley flakes to taste

1. Preheat oven to 350°F.
2. Coat a baking dish with low-calorie cooking spray. Place fillets in one layer in the dish. Sprinkle with salt, pepper, and paprika. Tightly cover dish with foil and bake for 20 to 25 minutes or until fish is cooked.
3. While fish is cooking, boil potatoes until tender.
4. In a small saucepan, combine butter and lemon juice. Heat until butter has melted.
5. Just before serving, transfer baked fish to a serving platter. Slice potatoes and arrange on the platter. Drizzle melted lemon butter evenly over fish and potatoes. Sprinkle with lemon pepper and parsley flakes and serve.

Serves 4
Approximately 9 grams fat per serving

SUGGESTED ACCOMPANIMENTS (see Index)

Green salad with Creamy Dijon
Baked Mélange
Rhubarb-Pineapple Compote

FLOUNDER MEUNIERE

Lightly floured, sautéed fillets of flounder topped with fresh lemon sauce and capers.

4 4-ounce flounder fillets
⅓ cup flour
Low-calorie cooking spray
2 tablespoons butter
2 tablespoons plus 1 teaspoon
  olive oil
Salt and pepper to taste
Garlic powder to taste
2 tablespoons fresh lemon juice
¼ cup water
1 tablespoon plus 1 teaspoon
  drained capers

1. Using a sifter, coat each piece of fish with flour. Set aside.

2. Coat a nonstick skillet with low-calorie cooking spray. Add butter and oil over medium-high heat. When butter has melted, add fish to skillet. Add salt, pepper, and garlic powder. Cook fish for 2 to 3 minutes, then turn fillets over. Cook for 3 to 4 minutes more or until fish is cooked. Remove fillets from skillet.

3. Add lemon juice and water to drippings in skillet. Cook for 1 minute over medium-high heat, stirring constantly.

4. Pour lemon sauce over fish. Top with capers and serve immediately.

Serves 4
Approximately 14.4 grams fat per serving

SUGGESTED ACCOMPANIMENTS (see Index)

Green salad with Zesty Lemon Vinaigrette
Asparagus with Delicate Mustard Sauce
Chocolate Crepes with Strawberries

FLOUNDER PARMESAN

Even friends who don't usually like the taste of fish have raved about this delicious dish.

Low-calorie cooking spray
4 4-ounce flounder fillets
½ teaspoon dried oregano leaves
Salt and pepper to taste
Dash garlic powder
¼ cup plus 2 tablespoons freshly
  grated Parmesan cheese
¼ cup chopped fresh parsley
⅛ teaspoon paprika
2 tablespoons plus 1 teaspoon
  butter, melted
2 cups hot cooked spaghetti

1. Preheat oven to 350°F.
2. Coat a baking dish with low-calorie cooking spray. Place fillets in one layer in the dish. Sprinkle with oregano, salt, pepper, and garlic powder. Tightly cover dish with foil and bake for 20 minutes or until fish is cooked. Transfer fish to a warm platter. Reset oven to broil.
3. In a small bowl, combine 2 tablespoons of the Parmesan, 2 tablespoons of the parsley, and paprika. Set aside.
4. Drizzle melted butter over fillets. Top with Parmesan mixture and broil, 2–3 inches from the heat source, for 1 to 2 minutes or until fillets have browned.
5. While fillets are broiling, toss hot spaghetti with remaining ¼ cup Parmesan and remaining 2 tablespoons parsley. Spoon onto a serving platter and top with fillets. Serve immediately.

Serves 4
Approximately 10.1 grams fat per serving

SUGGESTED ACCOMPANIMENTS (see Index)

Green salad with Italian's Italian
Squash Medley
Tropical Citrus Freeze

LINGUINE WITH CLAM SAUCE

Flavorful clams and mushrooms sautéed in olive oil and tossed with Romano cheese, pasta, and parsley.

Low-calorie cooking spray
2 tablespoons olive oil
1 teaspoon garlic powder
2 6½-ounce cans minced clams, well-drained
1 8-ounce can sliced mushrooms, drained
Salt and freshly ground pepper to taste
¼ cup chopped fresh parsley
2½ cups hot cooked linguine
¼ cup freshly grated Romano cheese

1. Coat a nonstick skillet with low-calorie cooking spray. Add 1 tablespoon of the olive oil and the garlic powder, clams, and mushrooms. Sauté over medium-high heat for 5 minutes. Remove skillet from heat.

2. Sprinkle salt, pepper, and parsley over clam and mushroom mixture. Add hot linguine and remaining tablespoon oil and toss well. Add cheese, toss again, and serve immediately.

Serves 4
Approximately 10.2 grams fat per serving

SUGGESTED ACCOMPANIMENTS (see Index)

Green salad with Italian's Italian
Broiled Tomatoes Dijon
Coconut Meringues with Pineapple Filling

MAIN COURSES
❧ BEEF ❧

BEEF ROASTED WITH GARLIC AND WINE

A highly flavored roast served in its own rich juices.

Low-calorie cooking spray
1¾ pounds boneless lean eye of
 round
1 medium-sized yellow onion,
 sliced
5 medium-sized cloves garlic,
 crushed
¼ cup burgundy
¼ cup canned or homemade beef
 broth
¼ cup water
Salt and pepper to taste

1. Preheat oven to 350°F.

2. Coat a skillet with low-calorie cooking spray. Place over high heat. When skillet is very hot, add meat and brown on both sides, being careful not to scorch. Transfer beef to a 1-quart casserole dish and set aside.

3. Reduce heat to medium and add onion and garlic to skillet. Sauté for 2 to 3 minutes. Add burgundy, broth, and water. Heat and pour mixture over beef. Sprinkle with salt and pepper.

4. Cover dish with aluminum foil and place lid on dish to seal it completely. Bake for 2 hours. Remove from oven and let stand for 10 minutes before slicing.

Serves 5
Approximately 8.2 grams fat per serving

SUGGESTED ACCOMPANIMENTS (see Index)

Green salad with Smooth and Creamy Blue
Baked Mélange
Strawberries in Vanilla Cream

GREEN PEPPER STEAK

Japanese-inspired fare—stir-fried beef with bell peppers, onion, tomatoes, and teriyaki sauce, served over rice.

Low-calorie cooking spray
⅔ pound boneless top round steak, cut into thin bite-sized pieces
1 cup sliced yellow onion
1½ large bell peppers, cut into strips
⅔ cup water
1 teaspoon beef bouillon granules
2 tablespoons teriyaki sauce
1 medium-sized clove garlic, minced
¼ cup water
1 tablespoon plus 1 teaspoon cornstarch
1½ medium-sized tomatoes, cut into bite-sized pieces
2 cups hot cooked white rice (no margarine added during cooking)

1. Coat a wok with low-calorie cooking spray. Add beef and brown over high heat. Remove beef and set aside.

2. Place onion in the wok. Reduce heat to medium-high and stir-fry until onion is tender and translucent (about 2 minutes). Add bell peppers, water, bouillon granules, teriyaki sauce, garlic, and beef. Reduce heat, cover wok, and simmer for 5 to 8 minutes or until meat is tender but thoroughly cooked.

3. In a small bowl, combine water and cornstarch. Pour mixture into wok and cook, stirring constantly, until sauce thickens. Add tomatoes and cook for 2 to 3 minutes more.

4. Place ½ cup rice on each of four individual serving plates. Spoon equal amounts of meat mixture over each rice serving.

Serves 4
Approximately 3.5 grams fat per serving

SUGGESTED ACCOMPANIMENTS (see Index)

Green salad with Chinatown Soy
Brown-Buttered Broccoli
Peaches and Cream with Nutmeg

BEEF BURGUNDY

Steak, mushrooms, onion, and parsley seasoned with thyme and rich red wine and spooned over egg noodles.

Low-calorie cooking spray
½ pound fresh mushrooms, sliced
¼ cup chopped yellow onion
¾ pound boneless lean top round steak, cut into thin strips
¼ cup chopped fresh parsley
1½ cups water
2 teaspoons beef bouillon granules
¼ teaspoon garlic powder
⅛ teaspoon pepper
⅛ teaspoon sugar
¼ teaspoon dried thyme leaves
1 small bay leaf
2 teaspoons cornstarch
2 tablespoons burgundy
2 cups hot cooked egg noodles

1. Coat a deep cooking pot or a Dutch oven with low-calorie cooking spray. Add mushrooms and onion and sauté over medium-high heat until brown (about 3 minutes). Remove from pot and set aside.

2. Place steak in pot and brown thoroughly over high heat (about 3 minutes). Add sautéed mushrooms and onion, parsley, water, bouillon granules, garlic powder, pepper, sugar, thyme, and bay leaf. Reduce heat, cover pot, and simmer for 1½ hours, stirring occasionally.

3. Combine cornstarch and burgundy. Mix well and add to pot. Cook for 5 to 10 minutes more. Remove bay leaf.

4. Place noodles in a 7″ × 11″ casserole dish. Spoon beef mixture over noodles and sprinkle with fresh parsley.

Serves 4
Approximately 4.2 grams fat per serving

SUGGESTED ACCOMPANIMENTS (see Index)

Green salad with Zesty Lemon Vinaigrette
Green Beans with Herbed "Butter"
Cherries in Champagne

HUNGARIAN GOULASH

A wonderfully flavored dish of beef, bacon, and vegetables served over a bed of noodles.

Low-calorie cooking spray
¾ pound boneless lean top round
   steak, cut into bite-sized pieces
¾ cup chopped yellow onion
½ cup condensed beef broth
½ cup undrained canned tomatoes
1¼ cups water
3 tablespoons chopped green bell
   pepper
1½ bacon strips, broiled until
   crisp, blotted dry, and chopped
1½ teaspoons paprika
½ teaspoon beef bouillon granules
¼ teaspoon salt
⅛ teaspoon pepper
¼ teaspoon dried marjoram leaves
2 cups hot cooked egg noodles

1. Coat a deep cooking pot or a Dutch oven with low-calorie cooking spray. Heat pot. Add beef and brown thoroughly over high heat (2 to 3 minutes). Reduce heat to medium-high, add onion and sauté until tender and translucent (2 to 3 minutes).

2. Add broth, tomatoes, water, bell pepper, bacon, paprika, bouillon granules, salt, pepper, and marjoram. Bring mixture to a boil, then reduce heat. Cover pot and simmer for 2 hours.

3. Place noodles on a serving platter. Spoon goulash over noodles and serve.

Serves 4
Approximately 5.3 grams fat per serving

SUGGESTED ACCOMPANIMENTS (see Index)

Green salad with Creamy Dijon
Butter-Glazed Carrots
Peaches and Cream with Nutmeg

SIMPLICITY

A sumptuous, slow-baked dish of beef, carrots, onion, and seasonings.

1 pound boneless lean top round
  steak, cut into bite-sized pieces
2 cups sliced carrots
1 medium-sized yellow onion,
  quartered
½ cup water
½ package dried French onion
  soup mix
Freshly ground pepper to taste

1. Preheat oven to 300°F.
2. Place steak, carrots, and onion in a 1½-quart casserole dish. Add water, soup mix, and pepper. Tightly cover dish with aluminum foil and bake for 3 hours. Don't peek! It's important to keep the dish tightly covered at all times during cooking.

Serves 4
Approximately 6.1 grams fat per serving

SUGGESTED ACCOMPANIMENTS (see Index)

Marinated Mushrooms with Blue Cheese
Cauliflower in Hot Cheese Sauce
Chocolate Crumb "Crème de Menthe"

ALL-AMERICAN BEEF STEW

This recipe is an old favorite of mine—a flavorful, guilt-free blend of beef and vegetables seasoned with a touch of thyme and garlic.

Low-calorie cooking spray
1 pound boneless lean chuck, cut into 1-inch cubes
2 cups canned or homemade beef broth
½ teaspoon paprika
½ teaspoon salt
¼ teaspoon pepper
⅛ teaspoon garlic powder
⅛ teaspoon ground thyme
¼ cup water
2 tablespoons cornstarch
¼ pound potato, peeled and diced
1 medium-sized yellow onion, cut into eighths
3 medium-sized stalks celery, diagonally sliced
3 medium-sized carrots, cut into julienne strips
2 medium-sized tomatoes, chopped
½ medium-sized green bell pepper, chopped
1 cup fresh green beans
2 tablespoons chopped fresh parsley

1. Coat a deep pot or a Dutch oven with low-calorie cooking spray. Heat pot. Place meat in pot and brown thoroughly over high heat (2 to 3 minutes).

2. Remove meat from pot and discard drippings. Return meat to pot and add broth, paprika, salt, pepper, garlic powder, and thyme. In a small jar, blend water and cornstarch. Add to pot, and bring mixture to a boil. Reduce heat, cover tightly, and simmer for 2 hours.

3. Place potato, onion, celery, carrots, tomatoes, bell pepper, and green beans in pot. Stir mixture and cook, covered, for 35 minutes more. Sprinkle with parsley and serve.

Serves 4
Approximately 7.1 grams fat per serving

SUGGESTED ACCOMPANIMENTS (see Index)

Green salad with Thousand Island Dressing
Broccoli with Delicate Mustard Sauce
Rhubarb-Pineapple Compote

MARINATED STEAK WITH HORSERADISH SAUCE

Juicy, thinly sliced steak served with a slightly spicy sauce of yogurt, horseradish, and mustard.

¼ cup oil-free Italian dressing
1 pound boneless top round steak
¼ cup plus 1 tablespoon plain
  nonfat yogurt
3 tablespoons low-calorie
  mayonnaise
1½ teaspoons prepared horseradish
½ teaspoon dry mustard
Salt and pepper to taste
1 teaspoon paprika
Garnish: Lemon wedges

1. Pour salad dressing over meat. Chill and marinate for at least 8 hours.

2. Preheat the broiler.

3. While meat is marinating, place yogurt, mayonnaise, horseradish, mustard, salt, and pepper in a small bowl. Mix well and set aside.

4. Remove steak from marinade and transfer steak to the rack of a broiling pan. Sprinkle with black pepper and ½ teaspoon of paprika. Broil, 2–3 inches away from the heat source, for about 3 minutes. Turn steak over, sprinkle with remaining paprika, and broil for 3 more minutes, or until cooked as desired. Slice into very thin strips and transfer to a serving platter. Garnish with lemon wedges and serve horseradish sauce on the side.

Serves 4 (2 tablespoons sauce per serving)
Approximately 16.2 grams fat per serving

SUGGESTED ACCOMPANIMENTS (see Index)

Marinated Mushrooms with Blue Cheese
Baked Squash Parmesan
Light Crepes with Apples and Cinnamon Sugar

BROILED STEAK IN HOT HONEY MUSTARD

An easy-to-make dish of marinated and broiled beef in a hot, sweet honey mustard sauce. This dish is also excellent when meat is grilled.

¼ cup Dijon mustard
3 tablespoons honey
12 drops hot sauce
⅓ teaspoon (1 packet) Equal
1 pound boneless top round steak

1. In a small bowl, combine mustard, honey, hot sauce, and Equal.
2. Place steak in a dish. Pour mustard mixture over meat and refrigerate for at least 8 hours.
3. Preheat the broiler.
4. Transfer steak to a broiling rack. Reserve marinade. Broil steak, 2–3 inches from the heat source, for 3 minutes. Turn steak over and broil for 3 more minutes, or until cooked as desired, basting frequently with mustard mixture.
5. Transfer steak to a serving platter. Cut into very thin slices and serve.

Serves 4
Approximately 6.3 grams fat per serving

SUGGESTED ACCOMPANIMENTS (see Index)

From a Corner of Chinatown
Cauliflower and Carrots with Nutmeg
Gingered Fruit in Plum Wine

BEEF KABOBS

Marinated steak and fresh mushrooms, skewered and broiled with crispy vegetables.

1¼ pounds boneless top round
   steak, cubed into 1-inch pieces
½ pound fresh mushrooms
1 cup teriyaki sauce
Freshly ground black pepper to
   taste
1 medium-sized yellow onion, cut
   into eighths
1 medium-sized green bell pepper,
   cut into bite-sized pieces
16 cherry tomatoes

1. Place steak and mushrooms in a casserole dish. Pour teriyaki sauce over them and sprinkle with black pepper. Refrigerate for at least 8 hours.
2. Preheat the broiler.
3. Remove meat and mushrooms from dish, discarding marinade. Thread steak, mushrooms, onion, bell pepper, and tomatoes on each of 8 skewers, alternating ingredients. Broil, 2–3 inches from heat source, turning frequently, 5 to 7 minutes, or until steak has cooked to desired doneness.

Serves 4
Approximately 9.3 grams fat per serving

SUGGESTED ACCOMPANIMENTS (see Index)

Green salad with Creamy Dijon
Cauliflower in Hot Cheese Sauce
Banana Cream Supreme

STEAK WITH ZESTY WHIPPED "BUTTER"

Lime-marinated steak, broiled and richly coated with mustard and Worcestershire in whipped "butter."

1¼ pounds boneless top round
  steak
1 tablespoon vegetable oil
¼ cup fresh lime juice
⅛ teaspoon garlic powder
Salt and pepper to taste
2 tablespoons plus 2 teaspoons
  low-calorie margarine
1 teaspoon dry mustard
2 teaspoons chopped fresh parsley
2 teaspoons Worcestershire sauce

1. Place steak in a casserole dish. Cover with oil, lime juice, garlic powder, salt, and pepper marinade. Refrigerate for at least 8 hours.

2. Preheat the broiler.

3. In a small bowl, combine margarine, mustard, parsley, and Worcestershire sauce. Mix well.

4. Lightly score steak with a knife. Transfer steak to a broiling pan and pour marinade over steak. Broil steak about 5 inches from heat source, about 3 minutes on each side, or until cooked as desired. Just before serving, spread "butter" mixture evenly over meat. Thinly slice steak and serve.

Serves 4
Approximately 12.8 grams fat per serving

SUGGESTED ACCOMPANIMENTS (see Index)

Green salad with Creamy Garlic with Parmesan
Mushrooms in Beef Burgundy Sauce
Chocolate Crepes with Strawberries

STUFFED CHEESEBURGERS

Everyone's favorite way to serve beef—without all those extra calories.

1 pound lean ground round
2 tablespoons skim milk
2 teaspoons Dijon mustard
1 teaspoon Worcestershire sauce
¼ teaspoon salt
⅛ teaspoon pepper
⅓ cup grated reduced-fat sharp cheddar cheese
3 tablespoons crumbled blue cheese
1 tablespoon plus 1 teaspoon finely chopped yellow onion
Chopped fresh parsley to taste
Low-calorie cooking spray

1. Preheat the broiler.
2. Mix together beef, skim milk, mustard, Worcestershire sauce, salt, and pepper. Form eight thin, evenly sized patties. Set aside.
3. Mix together cheddar and blue cheeses and onion. Sprinkle evenly onto four of the patties. Top with the remaining 4 patties so that the cheese and onion are in the middle. Press edges of top and bottom patties together to seal in cheese and onion. Sprinkle top patties with parsley.
4. Coat a broiling pan with low-calorie cooking spray and place the patties on the rack of the pan. Broil, 5 inches from heat source, for 3 minutes. Turn patties over and broil for 3 minutes more or until beef is cooked as desired.

Serves 4
Approximately 12.8 grams fat per serving

SUGGESTED ACCOMPANIMENTS (see Index)

Garden and Pasta Salad
Baked Mélange
Chocolate Dreams

SATURDAY'S MEAT LOAF

A moist, delectable, easy-to-make meat loaf. This is perfect for casual dining.

1¼ pounds lean ground round
¼ cup chopped celery
¼ cup chopped green bell pepper
¼ cup chopped yellow onion
¼ cup rolled oats
1 medium-sized egg white
1 tablespoon chopped fresh
  parsley
¾ teaspoon salt
¼ teaspoon pepper
1 8-ounce can tomato sauce

1. Preheat oven to 350°F.
2. In a mixing bowl, combine all ingredients, reserving half of the tomato sauce to put on top of the meat loaf.
3. Form mixture into an oval loaf. (Do *not* use a loaf pan.)
4. Place loaf on a rack of broiler pan and top with remaining tomato sauce. Place a shallow baking pan under the rack in the oven to catch drippings. Bake meat loaf for 45 to 50 minutes.

Serves 4
Approximately 10.3 grams fat per serving

SUGGESTED ACCOMPANIMENTS (see Index)

Green salad with Thousand Island Dressing
Mother's Cabbage
Baked Apples with Whipped Cream

HOT AND SPICY MEATBALL SOUP

This is a wonderful dish for cold, rainy nights—peppery meatballs in a rich beef broth, garnished with creamy yogurt.

1 pound lean ground round
2 slices "diet" bread, toasted and
  grated
¼ cup tomato sauce
3 small fresh hot green chilies,
  seeded and chopped fine
2 medium-sized egg whites, beaten
1 tablespoon chopped fresh
  parsley
1 teaspoon chili powder
1 teaspoon ground cumin
1 teaspoon salt
¼ teaspoon garlic powder
½ teaspoon dried oregano leaves
Low-calorie cooking spray
3 10-ounce cans condensed beef
  broth
1 quart water
¼ cup plain nonfat yogurt

1. Preheat the broiler.
2. In a mixing bowl, combine beef, bread crumbs, tomato sauce, chilies, egg whites, parsley, chili powder, cumin, salt, garlic powder, and oregano. Blend well and shape into 48 small meatballs (about 1-inch in diameter).
3. Coat a broiling pan with low-calorie cooking spray. Place meatballs on the rack of the pan and broil, 2–3 inches from the heat source, for 3 minutes. Turn each meatball over and broil for 3 minutes more or until thoroughly cooked. Remove from oven and place on paper towels to drain excess grease.
4. In a soup pot, heat broth and water. Bring to a boil, then add meatballs. Reduce heat and simmer for 10 minutes.
5. Divide broth and meatballs evenly among four individual serving bowls. Drizzle 1 tablespoon of yogurt over each serving.

Serves 4
Approximately 8 grams fat per serving

SUGGESTED ACCOMPANIMENTS (see Index)

Green salad with Creamy Avocado Dressing
Dilled Oven Fries
Five-Fruit Cup

MEATBALLS AND GRAVY

Hearty browned meatballs in a delicious beef gravy, served over mushroom-tossed rice.

2 tablespoons skim milk
¾ teaspoon cornstarch
¾ pound lean ground round
½ cup finely chopped yellow onion
1½ slices "diet" bread, toasted and grated
¼ teaspoon ground cumin
⅛ teaspoon garlic powder
Salt and pepper to taste
Low-calorie cooking spray
1¼ cups canned or homemade beef broth
1½ teaspoons cornstarch
1½ teaspoons flour
¼ pound fresh mushrooms, sliced
2 cups hot cooked white rice (no margarine added during cooking)

1. Preheat the broiler.
2. Combine skim milk and ¾ teaspoon cornstarch. Place in a large mixing bowl and add beef, onion, bread crumbs, cumin, garlic powder, salt, and pepper. Mix well and form into 32 small meatballs (about 1 inch in diameter).
3. Coat a broiling pan with low-calorie cooking spray. Place meatballs on the rack of the pan and broil, 2–3 inches from heat source, for 3 minutes. Turn each meatball over and broil for 3 minutes more or until thoroughly cooked.
4. While meatballs are broiling, combine broth, 1½ teaspoons cornstarch, and flour in a saucepan. Blend well and heat until slightly thickened.
5. Add meatballs to gravy and simmer, uncovered, for 10 minutes.
6. Coat a nonstick skillet with low-calorie cooking spray. Add mushrooms and sauté over medium-high heat for 3 minutes.
7. Toss rice and mushrooms together. Divide rice mixture evenly among four individual serving plates. Top each with eight meatballs and spoon an equal amount of gravy over each serving.

Serves 4
Approximately 6 grams fat per serving

SUGGESTED ACCOMPANIMENTS (see Index)

Lemon-Limed Tomatoes
Broccoli with Mild Lemon Curry Sauce
Five-Fruit Cup

CREAMY BEEF CASSEROLE WITH SCALLIONS

Luscious layers of noodles, cheese, scallions, and beef in a seasoned tomato sauce.

½ pound lean ground round
⅔ cup tomato sauce
1 teaspoon Worcestershire sauce
⅛ teaspoon sugar
¾ cup low-fat (1 percent fat)
  cottage cheese
3 scallions, chopped
Salt and pepper to taste
Dash cayenne pepper
2 cups cooked egg noodles
2 tablespoons chopped fresh
  parsley

1. Preheat oven to 350°F.
2. Brown beef in a nonstick skillet. Discard excess grease and place beef on paper towels to remove additional grease.
3. In a mixing bowl, combine beef, tomato sauce, Worcestershire sauce, and sugar. Set aside.
4. In a separate bowl, mix together cottage cheese, scallions, salt, pepper, and cayenne. Blend thoroughly.
5. Place cooked noodles in a 7" × 11" casserole dish. Top with cheese mixture, then add meat mixture. Sprinkle with parsley. Bake for 30 minutes and serve.

Serves 4
Approximately 4.4 grams fat per serving

SUGGESTED ACCOMPANIMENTS (see Index)

Green salad with Italian's Italian
Country Beans
Chocolate Meringue Puffs

SKILLET RIO GRANDE

A festive Mexican-inspired casserole of beef, tomatoes, onion, kidney beans, chili peppers, and seasonings, topped with a thin layer of cornmeal and sprinkled with cheese.

6 ounces lean ground round
2 medium-sized tomatoes, chopped
1 cup chopped yellow onion
½ cup drained canned kidney beans
1 fresh hot green chili, seeded and chopped fine
1 teaspoon chili powder
¾ teaspoon garlic salt
⅔ cup self-rising yellow cornmeal
¾ cup water
¼ teaspoon salt
½ cup grated reduced-fat sharp cheddar cheese

1. Preheat oven to 375°F.
2. Brown beef in a nonstick ovenproof skillet. Remove skillet from heat. Discard excess grease and place beef on paper towels to remove additional grease. Place beef back in skillet and add tomatoes, onion, kidney beans, fresh chili, chili powder, and garlic salt. Toss well.
3. In a bowl, combine cornmeal, water, and salt. Spoon over meat mixture to form a very thin top layer. Bake, uncovered, for 35 minutes.
4. Sprinkle cheese evenly over cornmeal topping. Bake for 5 minutes more and serve.

Serves 4
Approximately 6.4 grams fat per serving

SUGGESTED ACCOMPANIMENTS (see Index)

A Friend's Green Chili Salad
Broccoli with Delicate Mustard Sauce
Tropical Citrus Freeze

MOUSSAKA

A low-calorie version of a favorite Greek dish—savory beef, onion, eggplant, tomatoes, cinnamon, and allspice baked in a custard-type cream sauce.

Low-calorie cooking spray
1 small eggplant, peeled and sliced crosswise ½ inch thick
½ pound lean ground round
½ cup chopped yellow onion
¼ teaspoon garlic powder
½ cup chopped undrained canned tomatoes
¼ cup chopped fresh parsley
¼ teaspoon ground allspice
¾ teaspoon ground cinnamon
¼ teaspoon salt
⅛ teaspoon pepper
1 teaspoon sugar
1 medium-sized egg
¼ pound "light" cream cheese
½ cup plain nonfat yogurt

1. Preheat the broiler.
2. Coat a cookie sheet with low-calorie cooking spray. Place eggplant on sheet and broil, 5 inches from heat source, for 5 minutes. Turn each slice over and broil for 5 minutes more.
3. While eggplant is broiling, place beef, onion, and garlic powder in a nonstick skillet. Brown meat and discard excess grease. Place beef mixture on paper towels to remove additional grease. Place mixture back in skillet and add tomatoes, parsley, allspice, cinnamon, salt, pepper, and sugar. Mix together and simmer, uncovered, for 15 minutes.
4. Place eggplant in a 9-inch square casserole dish. Top with meat mixture. Reset oven to 350°F.
5. In a food processor fitted with the steel blade or a blender, place egg, cream cheese, and yogurt. Blend until smooth and pour over meat mixture. Bake for 30 minutes. Let stand for 5 minutes before serving.

Serves 4
Approximately 10.5 grams fat per serving

SUGGESTED ACCOMPANIMENTS (see Index)

Green salad with Sweet Basil Vinaigrette
Creamed Spinach
Dropped Strawberries

MEXICO'S FINEST SOUFFLE

An easy-to-make, subtly spicy soufflé of beef, onion, Mexican seasonings, chilies, and cheese.

⅔ pound lean ground round
¼ cup chopped yellow onion
½ teaspoon chili powder
¼ teaspoon dried oregano leaves
⅛ teaspoon garlic powder
⅛ teaspoon black pepper
⅛ teaspoon cayenne pepper
Low-calorie cooking spray
1 4-ounce can green chilies, drained
⅔ cup grated reduced-fat sharp cheddar cheese
1 cup skim milk
2 tablespoons flour
½ teaspoon salt
1 medium-sized egg, well beaten
2 medium-sized egg whites, well beaten

1. Preheat oven to 350°F.
2. In a nonstick skillet, brown beef and onion. Drain and discard excess grease. Place beef mixture on paper towels to remove additional grease.
3. Place beef and onion in a mixing bowl. Add chili powder, oregano, garlic powder, black pepper, and cayenne pepper. Stir well.
4. Coat a 9-inch square casserole dish with low-calorie cooking spray. Place chilies in dish. Top with cheese, then beef mixture. Set aside.
5. In a small bowl, combine skim milk, flour, salt, egg, and egg whites. Pour over meat mixture.
6. Place casserole dish securely in a shallow pan of hot water. The water should be at least 1 inch below the top of the casserole dish. Bake for 50 minutes. Let stand for 5 minutes before serving.

Serves 4
Approximately 10 grams fat per serving

SUGGESTED ACCOMPANIMENTS (see Index)

A Friend's Green Chili Salad
Baked Cloved Onions
Strawberries in Vanilla Cream

A FAMILY CASSEROLE

A quick and easy, truly satisfying main course dish. This is wonderful for days when you want a hot meal but don't have much time to spend in the kitchen.

⅔ **pound lean ground round**
Low-calorie cooking spray
1 medium-sized yellow onion,
    chopped
1 medium-sized green bell pepper,
    chopped
1 4-ounce can tomato sauce
2 teaspoons Worcestershire sauce
½ **teaspoon sugar**
Salt and pepper to taste
3 cups cooked egg noodles

1. Brown beef in a nonstick skillet. Drain and discard excess grease. Place beef on paper towels to remove additional grease.

2. Coat the skillet with low-calorie cooking spray. Add onion and bell pepper and sauté over medium-high heat until onion is translucent (about 4 minutes). Add beef, tomato sauce, Worcestershire sauce, sugar, salt, pepper, and noodles. Heat thoroughly and serve.

Serves 4
Approximately 5.3 grams fat per serving

SUGGESTED ACCOMPANIMENTS (see Index)

Green salad with Simply Blue
Country Beans
My Willie's Apples

BEEF STROGANOFF WITH DILL

A flavorful, rich stroganoff, mildly accented with dill and Dijon mustard.

Low-calorie cooking spray
½ cup chopped yellow onion
¼ teaspoon garlic powder
⅔ pound lean ground round
2 cups sliced fresh mushrooms
¾ cup condensed beef broth
1 tablespoon cornstarch
¼ teaspoon dried dill
1 cup plain nonfat yogurt
1 tablespoon Dijon mustard
2 cups hot cooked egg noodles
2 tablespoons chopped fresh
  parsley

1. Coat a skillet with low-calorie cooking spray. Heat skillet. Add onion and garlic powder and sauté over medium-high heat until onion is translucent (about 4 minutes). Add beef and mushrooms. Cook for 3 to 4 minutes, until beef is thoroughly done. Drain and discard excess grease. Place beef mixture on paper towels to remove additional grease. Place mixture back in skillet.

2. In a small jar, combine broth and cornstarch. Shake well to blend and add to beef mixture. Heat, stirring constantly, until sauce is smooth and thickened.

3. Remove skillet from heat. Stir in dill, yogurt, and mustard.

4. Toss together noodles and parsley. Place ½ cup noodle mixture on each of four individual serving plates. Top each serving with an equal amount of stroganoff.

Serves 4
Approximately 5 grams fat per serving

SUGGESTED ACCOMPANIMENTS (see Index)

Green salad with Creamy Dijon
Brown-Buttered Asparagus
Strawberries with Minted Chocolate

A LEBANESE FAVORITE

This is a very simple yet unique dish. The cinnamon and pecan pieces give it a slightly sweet flavor.

½ pound lean ground round
1½ cups chopped yellow onion
2 teaspoons ground cinnamon
2 teaspoons sugar
½ teaspoon ground allspice
¼ teaspoon salt
¼ cup pecan pieces
½ cup water
2 cups hot cooked white rice (no margarine added during cooking)

1. Brown beef in a nonstick skillet. Drain and discard excess grease. Place beef on paper towels to remove additional grease. Place beef back in skillet and add onion. Cook over medium heat until onion is translucent (5 to 7 minutes).

2. Reduce heat to medium-low. Add cinnamon, sugar, allspice, salt, and pecan pieces. Heat thoroughly.

3. Remove skillet from heat. Add water and stir. Cover skillet and let stand for 5 minutes.

4. Place ½ cup rice on each of four individual serving plates. Top each serving with an equal amount of beef mixture.

Serves 4
Approximately 9.5 grams fat per serving

SUGGESTED ACCOMPANIMENTS (see Index)

Green salad with Sweet Basil Vinaigrette
Creamed Spinach
Baked Pears in Orange-Raisin Sauce

EUNICE'S SWEDISH MEATBALLS

Lightly spiced meatballs in a tart pineapple sauce spooned over curried rice.

1 tablespoon plus 1 teaspoon skim
  milk
¾ teaspoon cornstarch
⅔ pound lean ground round
½ cup minced yellow onion
⅛ teaspoon garlic powder
⅛ teaspoon ground nutmeg
1 slice "diet" bread, toasted and
  grated
Salt and pepper to taste
Low-calorie cooking spray
⅔ cup undrained canned
  pineapple tidbits in their own
  juice
1½ teaspoons sugar
1½ teaspoons cornstarch
¾ teaspoon "lite" soy sauce
2 cups hot cooked white rice (no
  margarine added during
  cooking)
¼ teaspoon curry powder
3 tablespoons chopped scallion

1. Preheat the broiler.
2. Mix skim milk with ¾ teaspoon cornstarch. Add beef, onion, garlic powder, nutmeg, bread crumbs, salt, and pepper. Shape mixture into 28 small meatballs (1 inch in diameter).
3. Coat a broiling pan with low-calorie cooking spray. Place meatballs on the rack of the pan and broil, 2–3 inches from heat source, for 3 minutes. Turn each meatball over and broil for 3 minutes more or until thoroughly cooked.
4. While meatballs are broiling, place pineapple, sugar, and 1½ teaspoons cornstarch in a saucepan. Mix together and cook over medium-high heat until thickened. Stir in soy sauce.
5. Add meatballs to sauce. Remove from heat. Cover and let stand for 5 minutes.
6. In a separate bowl, combine rice, curry powder, and scallion. Toss well and place ½ cup rice mixture on each of four individual serving plates. Top each with seven meatballs and an equal amount of sauce and serve.

Serves 4
Approximately 5.1 grams fat per serving

SUGGESTED ACCOMPANIMENTS (see Index)

Waldorf Salad
Butter-Glazed Carrots
Banana Cream Supreme

BEEF AND GREEN CHILI CASSEROLE

Brimming with flavor, this casserole is sure to become one of your favorite low-calorie recipes.

½ pound lean ground round
½ cup chopped yellow onion
1 medium-sized green bell pepper, chopped
1 1-pound can chopped undrained tomatoes
1 teaspoon chili powder
½ teaspoon ground cumin
½ teaspoon ground coriander
½ teaspoon salt
¼ teaspoon garlic powder
⅛ teaspoon black pepper
⅛ teaspoon cayenne pepper
1½ cups cooked white rice (no margarine added during cooking)
3 tablespoons chopped scallion tops
¾ cup low-fat (1 percent fat) cottage cheese
2 tablespoons water
½ cup finely grated reduced-fat sharp cheddar cheese
1 4-ounce can green chilies, drained
Garnish: Cumin, black pepper, and chili powder

1. Preheat oven to 350°F.
2. Brown beef in a nonstick skillet. Drain and discard excess grease. Place beef on paper towels to remove additional grease. Place beef back in skillet and add onion and bell pepper. Sauté over medium-high heat until vegetables are tender but still crisp (3 to 4 minutes).
3. Add tomatoes, ½ teaspoon of the chili powder, cumin, coriander, salt, garlic powder, black pepper, and cayenne pepper. Simmer, uncovered, for 30 minutes.
4. While mixture is simmering, toss together rice, remaining ½ teaspoon chili powder, and scallion. Place rice mixture in a 7″ × 11″ casserole dish.
5. In a food processor fitted with the steel blade or a blender, combine cottage cheese and water. Blend until smooth. Spoon mixture over rice. Top with meat mixture, then cheddar cheese. Place chilies on top of cheese. Bake, uncovered, for 20 minutes or until thoroughly heated. Just before serving, sprinkle lightly with cumin and black pepper and liberally with chili powder.

Serves 4
Approximately 7.8 grams fat per serving

SUGGESTED ACCOMPANIMENTS (see Index)

A Friend's Green Chili Salad
The Grilled Onion
Tropical Citrus Freeze

PAN-FRIED STEAK WITH RED WINE SAUCE

A rich, distinctive sauce highlights this easy-to-prepare dish.

1½ teaspoons butter or margarine
1 tablespoon flour
1 tablespoon minced scallion
2 teaspoons finely chopped fresh
　parsley
1 small bay leaf
⅛ teaspoon sugar
⅔ cup condensed beef broth
1 tablespoon dry red wine
Low-calorie cooking spray
19 ounces boneless lean top round
　steak

1. Place butter or margarine in a saucepan. Melt over low heat. Stir in flour and gradually mix in scallion, parsley, bay leaf, sugar, broth, and wine. Increase heat to high and stir until sauce has thickened. Reduce heat to very low.

2. Coat a skillet with low-calorie cooking spray. Place over high heat. When skillet is quite hot, add steak. Brown for 2 to 3 minutes on each side or until cooked as desired. Transfer to a serving platter and slice in thin strips.

3. Remove bay leaf from sauce. Pour sauce evenly over steak and serve immediately.

Serves 4
Approximately 7.4 grams fat per serving

SUGGESTED ACCOMPANIMENTS (see Index)

Green salad with Zesty Lemon Vinaigrette
Baked Mélange
Strawberry-Crowned Lemon Chiffon

MAIN COURSES
❀ PORK ❀

SKILLET PORK

Nicely blended flavors of pork, browned rice, tomatoes, and green bell peppers.

Low-calorie cooking spray
1 pound pork tenderloin, cut into
   julienne strips
¼ cup water
6 tablespoons white rice,
   uncooked
1 large yellow onion, cut into 8
   slices
2 medium-sized tomatoes,
   trimmed and cut to make 4
   thick slices total
½ medium-sized green bell
   pepper, cut into 4 rings
1¼ cups condensed beef broth
¼ teaspoon dried marjoram leaves
¼ teaspoon dried thyme leaves

1. Preheat oven to 350°F.

2. Coat an ovenproof pot with low-calorie cooking spray. Heat the pot. Add pork and brown over high heat for 2 to 3 minutes. Set aside.

3. Pour water into pot. Boil for 1 minute, scraping the bottom and sides. Add rice and stir well. Place pork on top of rice. Top with onion slices, tomato slices, then bell pepper rings. Pour in broth and sprinkle in marjoram and thyme. Cover tightly and bake for 1 hour.

Serves 4
Approximately 4.1 grams fat per serving

SUGGESTED ACCOMPANIMENTS (see Index)

Creamy Cucumbers
Oven-Fried Okra
My Willie's Apples

SIMPLY PORK CHOPS

Nothing could be easier to prepare—broiled pork chops seasoned with robust garlic.

4 ½-inch-thick 5-ounce lean,
  boneless center-cut pork chops
¼ teaspoon garlic powder
2 teaspoons water
1 teaspoon paprika
Salt and pepper to taste

1. Preheat the broiler. Place pork chops on the rack of a broiling pan.

2. Mix together garlic powder and water. Spoon half of the mixture evenly over the pork chops. Sprinkle with ½ teaspoon paprika and salt and pepper. Broil, 2–3 inches from heat source, for 3 minutes. Turn pork chops over and cover with remaining garlic mixture and paprika. Broil for 3 to 4 minutes more or until pork chops are thoroughly cooked and nicely browned.

Serves 4
Approximately 11.3 grams fat per serving

SUGGESTED ACCOMPANIMENTS (see Index)

Old-Fashioned Coleslaw
Stewed Okra and Tomatoes
Baked Apples with Whipped Cream

CHINATOWN CABBAGE ROLLS

A delicate Oriental flavor gives these cabbage rolls their unique, mouth-watering taste.

Low-calorie cooking spray
¾ pound pork tenderloin, diced
4 scallions, chopped
½ pound fresh mushrooms, sliced
¼ pound fresh bean sprouts
2 tablespoons chopped red or
  green bell pepper
1 8-ounce can sliced water
  chestnuts, drained and chopped
1 cup cooked white rice (no
  margarine added during
  cooking)
1 cup canned or homemade beef
  broth
2 tablespoons "lite" soy sauce
⅛ teaspoon garlic powder
⅛ teaspoon ground ginger
Dash black pepper
½ cup water
4 large green cabbage leaves
1 tablespoon cornstarch

1. Preheat oven to 350°F.
2. Coat a nonstick skillet with low-calorie cooking spray. Heat skillet. Place pork and scallions in skillet and sauté over medium-high heat for 2 to 3 minutes until pork is lightly browned. Add mushrooms, bean sprouts, bell pepper, water chestnuts, rice, broth, soy sauce, garlic powder, ginger, and black pepper. Cover and simmer for 5 to 7 minutes or until vegetables are tender but still crisp. Drain, reserving liquid.
3. Pour water into a 2-quart pot or Dutch oven. Add cabbage leaves. Cover pot and simmer for 1 minute or until leaves are pliable. Transfer leaves to a platter.
4. Spoon ¼ cup meat mixture onto each leaf. Roll leaves up, tucking in the sides of each leaf. Place rolls, seam side down, in an 8" × 12" baking dish. Cover dish with foil and bake for 20 minutes.
5. While rolls are baking, place reserved liquid in a glass measuring cup. Add enough cold water to make 1 cup. Stir in cornstarch until smooth. Pour liquid into a saucepan and cook over high heat, stirring constantly, until sauce is thickened and bubbly (about 1 minute).
6. Remove cabbage rolls from oven and transfer to a serving platter. Pour sauce evenly over rolls and serve immediately.

Serves 4
Approximately 8 grams fat per serving

SUGGESTED ACCOMPANIMENTS (see Index)

Green salad with Sweet Honey Mustard Dressing
Carrots with Brown Sugar
Gingered Fruit in Plum Wine

PEPPERED PORK TENDERLOIN

Paper-thin slices of pork roast, heavily coated and roasted in fresh garlic and black pepper.

4 medium-sized cloves garlic,
    halved lengthwise
1½ pounds pork tenderloin roast
Freshly ground black pepper to
    taste
Seasoned salt to taste

1. Preheat oven to 350°F.
2. Thoroughly rub garlic cloves over roast. Cover roast with black pepper and sprinkle lightly with seasoned salt.
3. Place roast on a baking rack set over a pan to catch drippings. Bake for 50 to 55 minutes or until thoroughly cooked. Let stand for 10 minutes. Transfer to a serving platter and cut into very thin slices.

Serves 4
Approximately 7.2 grams fat per serving

SUGGESTED ACCOMPANIMENTS (see Index)

Tangy Cranberry Fiesta Salad
Mother's Cabbage
My Willie's Apples

SKEWERED PORK AND ORANGE CURRY

Pineapple-marinated pork, skewered with orange wedges and broiled in an orange and curry glaze. Do be sure to use the thinnest-skinned oranges you can find. When grilled, the entire orange pieces can be eaten.

1 pound boneless lean center-cut
    pork, cut into bite-sized pieces
¼ cup unsweetened pineapple
    juice
2 medium-sized thin-skinned
    oranges
¼ cup orange marmalade
2 tablespoons fresh orange juice
2 tablespoons water
¾ teaspoon curry powder
Low-calorie cooking spray

1. Place pork and pineapple juice in a glass bowl. Refrigerate for at least 3 hours.
2. Preheat the broiler.
3. Cut oranges into ½-inch-thick slices. Cut each slice into eight wedges. Thread equal amounts of pork and orange pieces onto four skewers, alternating meat and fruit pieces. Set aside.
4. In a saucepan, combine marmalade, orange juice, water, and curry powder. Heat until mixture is well blended and marmalade has melted.
5. Coat a broiling pan with low-calorie cooking spray. Place skewers on the rack of the pan and baste with marmalade mixture. Broil, 2–3 inches from heat source, for 5 to 7 minutes or until pork is thoroughly cooked, basting every 2 minutes.

Serves 4
Approximately 8.5 grams fat per serving

SUGGESTED ACCOMPANIMENTS (see Index)

Green salad with Chinatown Soy
Cauliflower and Carrots with Nutmeg
Coconut Meringues with Pineapple Filling

SZECHWAN PORK AND VEGETABLES

A highly seasoned medley of stir-fried pork, vegetables, garlic, and ginger.

1 tablespoon cornstarch
2 teaspoons fresh lime juice
2 teaspoons cooking sherry
2 tablespoons plus 1 teaspoon
    "lite" soy sauce
½ pound pork tenderloin, cut into
    bite-sized pieces
Low-calorie cooking spray
1½ teaspoons vegetable oil
2 cups broccoli flowerets
7 large fresh mushrooms, sliced
1 large green bell pepper, cut into
    strips
3 scallions, diagonally sliced
½ cup drained sliced water
    chestnuts
1½ teaspoons minced garlic
1½ teaspoons minced fresh
    gingerroot
1½ teaspoons hot red pepper flakes
⅓ cup water
2 cups hot cooked white rice (no
    margarine added during
    cooking)

1. In a small bowl, combine 1½ teaspoons of the cornstarch, lime juice, and sherry. Blend well. Mix in 1 tablespoon of the soy sauce and pour mixture over pork. Refrigerate for 15 minutes.

2. Coat a wok with low-calorie cooking spray. Pour in 1 teaspoon oil and turn heat medium-high. When oil is hot, add pork and marinade and stir-fry until pork is browned (about 3 to 5 minutes). Remove pork from wok and set aside.

3. Heat remaining ½ teaspoon oil in wok. Place broccoli, mushrooms, bell pepper, scallions, water chestnuts, garlic, gingerroot, and red pepper flakes in wok. Stir-fry over medium-high heat for 2 minutes. Reduce heat to medium, cover wok, and cook for 3 to 4 minutes until broccoli is tender but still crisp, stirring occasionally. Add pork and stir-fry for 2 minutes more.

4. In a separate bowl, combine water with remaining 1½ teaspoons cornstarch. Add remaining tablespoon plus 1 teaspoon soy sauce and pour mixture into wok. Cook for 1 to 2 minutes, stirring constantly, until sauce has thickened.

5. Place ½ cup rice on each of four individual serving plates. Spoon equal amounts of stir-fried mixture over each serving.

Serves 4
Approximately 4 grams fat per serving

SUGGESTED ACCOMPANIMENTS (see Index)

Fruited Melon Wedges
Brown-Buttered Asparagus
Baked Pears in Orange-Raisin Sauce

SKEWERED PORK WITH HONEY MUSTARD GLAZE

A hot, sweet honey mustard gives this main course dish its special flavor.

1 pound boneless lean center-cut
   pork, cut into bite-sized pieces
3 tablespoons Dijon mustard
3 tablespoons honey
8 drops hot sauce
Low-calorie cooking spray
1 medium-sized yellow onion, cut
   into eighths and separated
1 medium-sized green bell pepper,
   cut into chunks

1. Place pork in a glass bowl. In a separate bowl, combine mustard, honey, and hot sauce. Pour mixture over pork and refrigerate for at least 3 hours.
2. Preheat the broiler.
3. Coat four skewers with low-calorie cooking spray. Thread each skewer with one-quarter of the pork pieces, onion, and bell pepper, alternating ingredients. Place skewers on the rack of a broiling pan and baste with marinade. Broil, 2–3 inches from heat source, for 5 to 7 minutes or until pork is thoroughly cooked, basting frequently.

Serves 4
Approximately 8.3 grams fat per serving

SUGGESTED ACCOMPANIMENTS (see Index)

Mandarin Salad with Almonds
Cauliflower and Carrots with Nutmeg
Gingered Fruit in Plum Wine

PORK AND PEPPERS WITH PINEAPPLE RICE

A luscious, layered casserole of rice, sautéed pork with vegetables, and a slightly sweet pineapple sauce.

Low-calorie cooking spray
2 cups cooked white rice (no margarine added during cooking)
⅔ pound pork tenderloin, cut into julienne strips
1 medium-sized green bell pepper, cut into thin strips
1 tablespoon "lite" soy sauce
Salt and pepper to taste
3 tablespoons water
⅔ cup undrained canned crushed pineapple in its own juice
½ teaspoon grated orange zest
1 tablespoon dark brown sugar, not packed
⅓ teaspoon (1 packet) Equal
½ teaspoon ground cinnamon
½ cup water
2 teaspoons cornstarch

1. Preheat oven to 350°F.
2. Coat a casserole dish with low-calorie cooking spray. Place rice in dish. Set aside.
3. Place pork in a nonstick skillet. Sauté over high heat until nicely browned (2 to 3 minutes). Add bell pepper, soy sauce, salt, and pepper. Cook until bell pepper is tender but still crisp (about 2 minutes), stirring constantly. Add 3 tablespoons water and stir.
4. Place meat mixture on top of rice.
5. In a small saucepan, combine pineapple, orange zest, brown sugar, Equal, and cinnamon. In a separate bowl, combine ½ cup water and cornstarch. Add to mixture in saucepan and cook for 2 to 3 minutes, or until slightly thickened. Spoon sauce over meat and bell pepper mixture. Bake, uncovered, for 20 minutes.

Serves 4
Approximately 3 grams fat per serving

SUGGESTED ACCOMPANIMENTS (see Index)

Green salad with Creamy Dijon
Baked Cloved Onions
Baked Pears in Orange-Raisin Sauce

MAIN COURSES
❧ MEATLESS ❧

LINGUINE AND VEGETABLES

Fresh tomatoes, black olives, and Parmesan cheese give this pasta dish its fresh, delicious flavor.

5½ ounces linguine
Low-calorie cooking spray
1½ cups thinly sliced zucchini
½ pound fresh mushrooms, sliced thin
⅓ cup chopped yellow onion
2 tablespoons chopped fresh parsley
¾ teaspoon garlic powder
½ teaspoon dried basil leaves
½ teaspoon dried oregano leaves
Salt and pepper to taste
3 medium-sized tomatoes, chopped
¼ cup sliced pitted black olives
⅓ cup freshly grated Parmesan cheese

1. Break lingine in half and boil until al dente.
2. While linguine is cooking, coat a nonstick Dutch oven with low-calorie cooking spray. Add zucchini, mushrooms, onion, parsley, garlic powder, basil, oregano, salt, and pepper. Sauté over medium-high heat until onion is translucent (4 to 5 minutes).
3. Drain linguine and add to vegetables. Mix in tomatoes and olives. Toss well and heat thoroughly. Just before serving, toss with Parmesan cheese.

Serves 4
Approximately 4.2 grams fat per serving

SUGGESTED ACCOMPANIMENTS (see Index)

Green salad with Zesty Lemon Vinaigrette
Brown-Buttered Asparagus
Tropical Citrus Freeze

CREAM CHEESE AND NOODLES WITH SCALLIONS

A rich and creamy meatless casserole full of creamed cheese, zesty scallions, and light egg noodles.

⅓ cup low-fat (1 percent fat) cottage cheese
3 ounces light cream cheese
⅓ cup plain nonfat yogurt
¼ teaspoon salt
⅛ teaspoon pepper
3½ cups cooked egg noodles
⅓ cup chopped scallion

1. Preheat oven to 350°F.
2. In a food processor fitted with the steel blade or a blender, combine cottage cheese, cream cheese, yogurt, salt, and pepper. Blend well.
3. Toss together noodles and scallion. Add cheese mixture and stir thoroughly. Place in a 7″ × 11″ casserole dish and bake, covered, for 20 minutes.

Serves 4
Approximately 7.4 grams fat per serving

SUGGESTED ACCOMPANIMENTS (see Index)

Green salad with Zesty Lemon Vinaigrette
Peas and Water Chestnuts
Coconut Meringues with Pineapple Filling

TRIPLE-CHEESE LASAGNA

Lasagna noodles, a hearty sauce, and three delicious cheeses layered and baked to perfection.

Low-calorie cooking spray
½ teaspoon olive oil
2 medium-sized cloves garlic,
   minced
½ cup chopped yellow onion
1 cup undrained canned tomatoes
⅓ cup tomato paste
2 tablespoons chopped fresh
   parsley
¼ teaspoon dried oregano leaves
¼ teaspoon dried basil leaves
¼ teaspoon fennel seeds
1 cup water
Salt and pepper to taste
4 lasagna noodles, cooked
¾ cup low-fat (1 percent fat)
   cottage cheese
1 cup shredded mozzarella cheese
¼ cup freshly grated Parmesan
   cheese

1. Preheat oven to 350°F.
2. Coat a nonstick skillet with low-calorie cooking spray. Add oil and heat. Add garlic and onion and sauté over medium-high heat until onion is translucent (2 to 3 minutes). Add tomatoes, tomato paste, parsley, oregano, basil, fennel seeds, water, salt, and pepper. Simmer, uncovered, for 25 minutes.
3. While sauce is simmering, boil noodles.
4. Place two lasagna noodles flat in a 7″ × 11″ casserole dish. Top with half of the sauce, then spoon on half of the cottage cheese. Add ¼ cup of the mozzarella cheese. Repeat the layers. Top with Parmesan and remaining mozzarella cheeses and bake for 30 minutes or until cheese has melted. Let stand for 5 minutes before serving.

Serves 4
Approximately 7.6 grams fat per serving

SUGGESTED ACCOMPANIMENTS (see Index)

Europe's Pride
Zucchini Toss
Strawberry Sorbet

THE OVERLOADED PIZZA

Here's a wonderful way to have your pizza—meat- and guilt-free!

¾ cup tomato sauce
Salt and pepper to taste
¼ teaspoon dried oregano leaves
¼ teaspoon fennel seeds
⅛ teaspoon garlic powder
Low-calorie cooking spray
½ cup chopped yellow onion
½ cup chopped green bell pepper
½ pound fresh mushrooms, sliced
⅓ cup thinly sliced zucchini
2 6-inch whole-wheat pocket pita
  bread
16 small pitted black olives, sliced
1 cup shredded mozzarella cheese
¼ cup freshly grated Parmesan
  cheese
Freshly ground black pepper to
  taste
Hot red pepper flakes to taste

1. In a small bowl, combine tomato sauce, salt, pepper, oregano, fennel seeds, and garlic powder.

2. Preheat oven to 400°F.

3. Coat a skillet with low-calorie cooking spray. Add onion, bell pepper, mushrooms and zucchini. Sauté over medium-high heat until onion is translucent (about 3 minutes).

4. Separate each pita, forming 4 rounds of bread. Place pita rounds on a nonstick cookie sheet. Spoon 3 of the tablespoons seasoned tomato sauce onto each round. Place one-quarter of the olive slices and an equal amount of vegetables on each round. Top each with ¼ cup mozzarella cheese.

5. Bake for 10 minutes or until cheese is bubbly and lightly browned. Sprinkle 1 tablespoon Parmesan cheese over each pizza and top with freshly ground black pepper and red pepper flakes.

Serves 4
Approximately 9 grams fat per serving

SUGGESTED ACCOMPANIMENT (see Index)

Green salad with Zesty Lemon Vinaigrette
Green Beans with Herbed "Butter"
Chocolate-Drizzled Fruit Kabobs

THE DECADENT CRUSTLESS QUICHE

A sumptuous, generously portioned dish of eggs, three cheeses, and garden-fresh vegetables.

5 medium-sized eggs
¼ cup skim milk
⅓ cup grated reduced-fat sharp
  cheddar cheese
⅓ cup grated Monterey Jack cheese
  with jalapeño pepper
⅓ cup grated mozzarella cheese
Low-calorie cooking spray
⅓ cup chopped yellow onion
¼ cup thinly sliced green bell
  pepper
1 cup thinly sliced fresh
  mushrooms
Salt and pepper to taste
¼ teaspoon chili powder
⅛ teaspoon cayenne pepper
⅛ teaspoon garlic powder
6 medium-sized pitted black
  olives, sliced thin
1 medium-sized tomato, chopped
1 tablespoon freshly grated
  Parmesan cheese
3 tablespoons chopped fresh
  parsley
Paprika

1. Preheat oven to 350°F.
2. In a small bowl, combine eggs and skim milk. Beat well and stir in cheddar, Monterey Jack, and mozzarella cheeses. Set aside.
3. Coat a nonstick skillet with low-calorie cooking spray. Heat skillet. Add mushrooms and sauté over high heat. Add onions and bell pepper and sauté 1 to 2 minutes, stirring constantly. Remove from heat. Add olives, tomatoes, salt, pepper, chili powder, cayenne pepper, and garlic powder. Stir thoroughly, cover, and let stand 2 minutes.
4. Spoon vegetables into a 9-inch pie pan. Pour egg mixture evenly over vegetables. Top with Parmesan cheese, parsley, and paprika.
5. Bake for 35 to 40 minutes or until center of pie is set. Let stand for 5 minutes before serving.

Serves 4
Approximately 14 grams fat per serving

SUGGESTED ACCOMPANIMENTS (see Index)

Green salad with Sweet Basil Vinaigrette
Broiled Tomatoes Dijon
Blueberries and Wine

CREAMY CHEESE QUICHE

A sensational dish of eggs, three cheeses, hot peppers, fresh vegetables, and seasonings.

5 medium-sized eggs
¼ cup skim milk
⅓ cup grated reduced-fat cheddar cheese
⅓ cup grated Monterey Jack cheese with jalapeño pepper
⅓ cup grated reduced-fat Swiss cheese
Low-calorie cooking spray
⅓ cup finely chopped yellow onion
1 cup thinly sliced fresh mushrooms
½ teaspoon Cajun seasoning
1 medium-sized tomato, chopped
1½ cups cooked bite-sized cauliflower flowerets
Salt and pepper to taste
Dash cayenne pepper
1 tablespoon freshly grated Parmesan cheese
3 tablespoons chopped fresh parsley
Paprika

1. Preheat oven to 350°F.
2. In a small bowl, combine eggs and skim milk. Beat well and stir in cheddar, Monterey Jack, and Swiss cheeses. Set aside.
3. Coat a nonstick skillet with low-calorie cooking spray. Add onion and sauté over medium heat for 2 to 3 minutes until translucent. Add mushrooms and Cajun seasoning. Cook over medium heat until mushrooms are browned (2 to 3 minutes). Add tomato, cauliflower, salt, pepper, and cayenne pepper and cook for 1 minute more.
4. Coat a 9-inch pie pan with low-calorie cooking spray. Place vegetable mixture in pan. Pour egg mixture over vegetables and top with Parmesan cheese, parsley, and paprika. Bake for 25 to 35 minutes or until center of quiche is set. Let stand for 5 minutes before serving.

Serves 4
Approximately 14 grams fat per serving

SUGGESTED ACCOMPANIMENTS (see Index)

Green salad with Creamy Dijon
Brown-Buttered Asparagus
Blueberry and Lime Sorbet

INDIVIDUAL REFRIED BEAN CASSEROLES

Spicy seasoned refried beans covered with cheese and layered with fresh onion, sweet bell pepper, tomato, and lettuce.

2½ cups drained canned pinto beans (reserve liquid)
¼ teaspoon garlic powder
½ teaspoon chili powder
6 drops hot sauce
Low-calorie cooking spray
1 cup grated reduced-fat cheddar cheese
½ cup chopped yellow onion
½ cup finely chopped green bell pepper
1 large tomato, chopped
4 cups shredded lettuce
½ cup picante sauce
Salt and pepper to taste

1. Preheat oven to 350°F.
2. Place beans, garlic powder, chili powder, and hot sauce in a mixing bowl. Mash until mixture is smooth and well blended, adding reserved liquid from beans as necessary to achieve a creamy consistency.
3. Coat four individual gratin dishes with low-calorie cooking spray. Spoon ½ cup bean mixture into each dish. Top with cheese and bake for 20 minutes or until cheese is bubbly.
4. Top each dish with an equal amount of onion, bell pepper, tomato, and lettuce. Drizzle 2 tablespoons picante sauce over each dish. Salt and pepper to taste and serve.

Serves 4
Approximately 5.5 grams fat per serving

SUGGESTED ACCOMPANIMENTS (see Index)

Spicy Peaches
Oven-Fried Okra
Banana Cream Supreme

ORIENTAL STUFFED PITAS

Whole-wheat pita halves filled with crunchy stir-fried vegetables—an Oriental-flavored delight.

1 tablespoon peanut oil
¾ teaspoon freshly grated gingerroot
1 cup broccoli flowerets
1 cup cauliflower flowerets
1 cup slivered yellow onion
1 cup diagonally sliced celery
1 cup chopped fresh green beans
1 8-ounce can sliced water chestnuts, drained
1 cup water
2 teaspoons chicken bouillon granules
½ teaspoon hot red pepper flakes
¼ teaspoon garlic powder
1 tablespoon plus 1 teaspoon cornstarch
4 6-inch whole-wheat pocket pita bread, halved and warmed
½ cup alfalfa sprouts
1 medium-sized tomato, chopped
⅓ medium-sized green bell pepper, chopped
⅓ cup chopped scallion
1 cup shredded lettuce
2 tablespoons "lite" soy sauce

1. Heat oil in a wok over medium-high heat. Add gingerroot and stir-fry for 30 seconds. Add broccoli, cauliflower, onion, celery, green beans, and water chestnuts and stir-fry for 3 minutes. Reduce heat to medium, cover wok, and cook for 3 to 4 minutes longer, stirring occasionally.

2. In a small bowl, combine water, bouillon granules, red pepper flakes, garlic powder, and cornstarch. Pour cornstarch mixture into wok and toss well. Remove wok from heat.

3. Spoon an equal amount of vegetable mixture into each pita half. Top each with equal amounts of alfalfa sprouts, tomato, bell pepper, scallion, and lettuce. Drizzle 1½ teaspoons soy sauce over each sandwich and serve.

Serves 4
Approximately 4.8 grams fat per serving

SUGGESTED ACCOMPANIMENTS (see Index)

Green salad with Chinatown Soy
Asparagus with Delicate Mustard Sauce
Cherries in Champagne

ZUCCHINI AND CHEESE CASSEROLE

A delicious, easy-to-prepare dish of zucchini, onion, and thyme blended with eggs, cheese, and savory seasonings.

3 cups grated zucchini
1 medium-sized yellow onion, grated
1 large clove garlic, grated
1 teaspoon salt
¼ teaspoon pepper
2 medium-sized eggs, slightly beaten
3 tablespoons flour
⅛ teaspoon ground thyme
2 tablespoons chopped fresh parsley
1 or 2 dashes cayenne pepper, if desired
1 cup grated reduced-fat cheddar cheese

1. Preheat oven to 350°F.
2. Mix together all ingredients except ½ cup of the cheddar cheese. Place mixture in a casserole dish and bake for 25 minutes.
3. Sprinkle remaining ½ cup cheddar cheese on top of mixture and bake for 5 minutes more. Let stand for 5 minutes before serving.

Serves 4
Approximately 8.3 grams fat per serving

SUGGESTED ACCOMPANIMENTS (see Index)

Green salad with Creamy Dijon
Cauliflower and Carrots with Nutmeg
Tropical Lemon Cream Squares

ASPARAGUS AND VEGETABLE CASSEROLE

A delightfully rich, garden-fresh casserole of rice, vegetables, and cheese.

6 ounces fresh green beans,
  quartered lengthwise
½ pound fresh or frozen petite
  peas
½ pound fresh asparagus
¼ pound fresh mushrooms, sliced
¼ cup finely chopped celery
2 tablespoons finely chopped
  yellow onion
1 cup cooked white rice (no
  margarine added during
  cooking)
1 10-ounce can undiluted
  condensed cream of celery soup
⅔ cup grated reduced-fat sharp
  cheddar cheese
30 Cheez-It cheese crackers,
  crumbled coarse

1. Lightly steam green beans, fresh peas, and asparagus until tender but still crisp. (If you are using frozen peas, just thaw them.)

2. Preheat oven to 350°F.

3. Place green beans in a 7″ × 11″ casserole dish. Add, in layers, peas, asparagus, mushrooms, celery, onion, and rice. Spoon soup over rice. Top first with cheese, then with crumbled crackers.

4. Bake, uncovered, for 30 minutes. Serve immediately.

Serves 4
Approximately 7.9 grams fat per serving

SUGGESTED ACCOMPANIMENTS (see Index)

Carrot and Bell Pepper Salad
A Finely Broiled Tomato
Rhubarb-Pineapple Compote

SAUTEED CABBAGE WITH NOODLES

Shredded cabbage, sautéed to a rich golden brown and tossed with egg noodles—a satisfying, easy-to-make, economical dish.

Low-calorie cooking spray
1 tablespoon plus 2 teaspoons
  butter or margarine
8 cups shredded green cabbage
Salt and pepper to taste
3 cups hot cooked egg noodles

1. Coat a Dutch oven with low-calorie cooking spray. Add butter or margarine and heat until bubbly.

2. Add cabbage and sauté over medium-high heat until edges are nicely browned and cabbage is tender (about 15 minutes). Add salt and pepper to taste.

3. Place noodles in a serving bowl. Add cabbage and toss well. Serve immediately.

Serves 4
Approximately 5.5 grams fat per serving

SUGGESTED ACCOMPANIMENTS (see Index)

Green salad with Smooth and Creamy Blue
Tomato Casserole
Rhubarb-Pineapple Compote

PIE PARMESAN

Sautéed and seasoned Italian vegetables spooned over a baked Parmesan pie crust, topped with mozzarella cheese.

1½ cups cooked brown rice (no margarine added during cooking)

⅔ cup freshly grated Parmesan cheese

Low-calorie cooking spray

1 teaspoon olive oil

½ cup chopped yellow onion

½ medium-sized bell pepper, chopped

1 medium-sized clove garlic, minced

1½ cups chopped zucchini

1 medium-sized tomato, chopped

1 tablespoon chopped fresh parsley

½ teaspoon dried oregano leaves

¼ teaspoon salt

½ bay leaf

⅛ teaspoon black pepper

1 cup shredded mozzarella cheese

1. Preheat oven to 350°F.

2. Mix together rice and Parmesan cheese. Place in a 9-inch pie pan and pat bottom and sides down firmly. Bake for 20 to 25 minutes or until lightly browned.

3. While crust is baking, coat a nonstick skillet with low-calorie cooking spray. Add oil and heat. Add onion, bell pepper, and garlic and sauté over medium-high heat until vegetables are tender but still crisp (2 to 3 minutes). Add zucchini.

4. Add tomato, parsley, oregano, salt, bay leaf, and pepper. Tightly cover skillet, reduce heat to low, and simmer for 20 minutes. Remove and discard bay leaf.

5. Spoon vegetable mixture into crust. Top with mozzarella and bake for 5 minutes. Let stand for 5 minutes before serving.

Serves 4
Approximately 10.2 grams fat per serving

SUGGESTED ACCOMPANIMENTS (see Index)

Green salad with Simply Blue
Broiled Tomatoes Dijon
Chocolate-Drizzled Fruit Kabobs

RAINY DAY BROCCOLI SOUP
WITH JALAPEÑO CORN MUFFINS

A hearty cream soup, full of broccoli bits and a hint of nutmeg. Serve this with Jalapeño Corn Muffins (recipe follows).

Soup
2 10-ounce packages frozen
  broccoli spears
1 quart water
Low-calorie cooking spray
⅔ cup chopped yellow onion
⅔ cup chopped celery
1 cup undiluted condensed cream
  of celery soup
⅔ cup evaporated skim milk
2 cups canned or homemade
  chicken broth
2 tablespoons chopped fresh
  parsley
¼ teaspoon ground nutmeg
Salt and pepper to taste

1. Place broccoli and water in a Dutch oven. Cook broccoli for 8 to 10 minutes or until tender.
2. While broccoli is cooking, coat a nonstick skillet with low-calorie cooking spray. Heat skillet. Add onion and celery and sauté over medium-high heat until onion is translucent (2 to 3 minutes).
3. Remove broccoli, reserving liquid in Dutch oven. Cut stems from broccoli. Set aside flowerets and place stems in a blender or food processor fitted with the steel blade. Blend at a high speed until stems are fairly well pureed (1 to 2 minutes). Coarsely chop flowerets.
4. Place broccoli puree and chopped flowerets, onion, celery, and all other ingredients in Dutch oven. Cover and simmer over low heat for 10 minutes.

Serves 4
Approximately 2.2 grams fat per serving

Jalapeño Corn Muffins
1⅓ cups yellow cornmeal
1¾ cups buttermilk
⅓ cup self-rising flour
1 medium-sized egg white
¼ teaspoon salt
1 medium-sized jalapeño pepper,
  seeded and chopped fine
Low-calorie cooking spray

1. Preheat oven to 400°F.
2. In a mixing bowl, combine all ingredients except cooking spray. Stir until smooth.
3. Coat an 8-cup nonstick muffin tin with low-calorie cooking spray. Divide batter evenly among cups and bake for 25 minutes.

Serves 8
Approximately 0.7 grams fat per serving

Note: Corn muffins may be wrapped in foil and frozen for up to 2 weeks.

SUGGESTED ACCOMPANIMENTS (see Index)

Green salad with Zesty Lemon Vinaigrette
A Finely Broiled Tomato
Chocolate-Drizzled Fruit Kabobs

TORTILLA SOUP WITH CILANTRO

A zesty tomato-, chicken-, and beef-based soup flavored with hot chilies, cheese, cilantro, and tortilla strips.

1 tablespoon plus 1 teaspoon
   vegetable oil
⅓ cup chopped yellow onion
1 fresh hot green chili, minced
   fine
3 medium-sized cloves garlic,
   minced
1½ cups peeled chopped tomatoes
1⅔ cups canned or homemade
   beef broth
1⅔ cups canned or homemade
   chicken broth
2 cups water
2 cups tomato juice
⅔ cup fresh or frozen corn kernels
1½ teaspoons ground cumin
1½ teaspoons chili powder
1¼ teaspoons salt
⅛ teaspoon pepper
2 teaspoons Worcestershire sauce
1 tablespoon bottled steak sauce
2 6-inch flour tortillas, cut in half
   and then cut into ⅛-inch strips
2 tablespoons finely chopped
   cilantro
½ cup grated reduced-fat sharp
   cheddar cheese
½ cup grated Monterey Jack with
   jalapeño peppers

1. Place oil in a large Dutch oven (preferably iron). Add onion, green chili, and garlic. Sauté over medium heat until onion is translucent (1 to 2 minutes). Add all remaining ingredients except tortillas, cilantro, and cheeses.

2. Bring mixture to a boil. Reduce heat and simmer, covered, for 1 hour.

3. Just before serving, add tortilla strips and cilantro to soup. Stir well, pour into bowls, and top with cheddar and Monterey Jack cheeses.

Serves 4
Approximately 10.2 grams fat per serving

SUGGESTED ACCOMPANIMENTS (see Index)

Green salad with Creamy Avocado Dressing
Butter-Glazed Carrots
Tropical Citrus Freeze

SPINACH- AND CHEESE-STUFFED MANICOTTI

A rich, zesty Italian dish of pasta, spinach, and cheeses.

1½ cups tomato sauce
1¼ cups water
½ cup chopped yellow onion
½ teaspoon dried basil leaves
½ teaspoon fennel seeds
¼ teaspoon dried oregano leaves
½ teaspoon salt
¼ teaspoon garlic powder
¼ teaspoon pepper
8 manicotti shells
1½ cups chopped drained cooked
   spinach
¾ cup low-fat (1 percent fat)
   cottage cheese
¼ cup plus 1 tablespoon freshly
   grated Parmesan cheese
¼ cup chopped fresh parsley

1. Preheat oven to 350°F.
2. In a pot, combine tomato sauce, water, onion, basil, fennel, oregano, ¼ teaspoon of the salt, garlic powder, and pepper. Cover and simmer for 1 hour.
3. Boil manicotti shells until al dente. Meanwhile, mix together spinach, cottage cheese, Parmesan cheese, and remaining ¼ teaspoon salt.
4. Stuff each shell with an equal amount of spinach mixture. Place shells in an 8″ × 12″ casserole dish. Pour sauce evenly over shells.
5. Bake for 35 minutes. Top with parsley and serve.

Serves 4
Approximately 3.6 grams fat per serving

SUGGESTED ACCOMPANIMENTS (see Index)

Green salad with Sweet Basil Vinaigrette
Green Beans with Herbed "Butter"
Frozen Sugar-Coated Grapes

CHEESY ONION CASSEROLE

A hearty casserole of three cheeses, eggs, and spices.

Low-calorie cooking spray
4 cups thinly sliced yellow onion
⅓ cup grated reduced-fat Swiss
   cheese
⅓ cup grated reduced-fat cheddar
   cheese
1¼ cups low-fat (1 percent fat)
   cottage cheese
2 medium-sized eggs
¾ teaspoon salt
⅛ teaspoon ground nutmeg
Dash black pepper
20 Cheez-It cheese crackers,
   crumbled coarse
Paprika

1. Preheat oven to 350°F.
2. Coat a nonstick skillet with low-calorie cooking spray. Place over medium-high heat and add onion. Sauté for 5 to 7 minutes until onion is a golden brown.
3. Transfer onion to a 9-inch square casserole dish. Top with Swiss and cheddar cheeses.
4. In a blender or a food processor fitted with the steel blade, place cottage cheese, eggs, salt, nutmeg, and black pepper. Blend until smooth and pour over cheeses. Top with cracker crumbs and sprinkle with paprika.
5. Bake for 35 minutes.

Serves 4
Approximately 8.6 grams fat per serving

SUGGESTED ACCOMPANIMENTS (see Index)

Old-Fashioned Coleslaw
All-American Oven Fries
Ambrosia

PLAIN AND SIMPLE 250-CALORIE MAIN-COURSE DISHES

When there's no time to create a more elaborate entree, these quick-fix main courses will keep you right on track with your diet.

POULTRY

Chicken: 5⅓ ounces (1¼ cups chopped) skinless roasted breast meat equal one 250-calorie serving. Approximately 5.5 grams fat per serving.
Turkey: 5½ ounces (1⅓ cups chopped) skinless roasted white meat equal one 250-calorie serving. Approximately 5 grams fat per serving.
Turkey Ham: 6¾ ounces (1½ cups chopped) cured thigh meat equal one 250-calorie serving. Approximately 9.5 grams fat per serving.

SEAFOOD

Crab Meat: 8⅔ ounces (1¼ cups) cooked equal one 250-calorie serving. Approximately 4.3 grams fat per serving.
Flounder: 12 ounces raw equal one 250-calorie serving. Approximately 1.8 grams fat per serving.
Halibut: 8 ounces raw equal one 250-calorie serving. Approximately 5.3 grams fat per serving.
Oysters: 22 medium-sized raw equal one 250-calorie serving. Approximately 6 grams fat per serving.
Perch: 10 ounces raw equal one 250-calorie serving. Approximately 2.6 grams fat per serving.
Shrimp: 9.6 ounces (1¼ cups) peeled and boiled equal one 250-calorie serving. Approximately 2.1 grams fat per serving.

BEEF

Flank Steak: 3⅔ ounces broiled equal one 250-calorie serving. Approximately 15.4 grams fat per serving.
Hamburger: 4⅓ ounces lean broiled ground round equal one 250-calorie serving. Approximately 10.8 grams fat per serving.
Top Round Steak: 4½ ounces broiled equal one 250-calorie serving. Approximately 7.6 grams fat per serving.
Eye of Round Roast: 4¾ ounces roasted equal one 250-calorie serving. Approximately 8.5 grams fat per serving.

PORK

Center-Cut: 3⅔ ounces boneless roasted meat equal one 250-calorie serving. Approximately 13.6 grams fat per serving.
Tenderloin: 5⅓ ounces roasted equal one 250-calorie serving. Approximately 6.8 grams fat per serving.

6
✤ VEGETABLES ✤

BROWN-BUTTERED ASPARAGUS

Steamed fresh asparagus is a treat anytime, but especially when served in a rich, nutty-flavored brown butter.

1 pound fresh asparagus
2½ teaspoons butter
Dash garlic powder
½ teaspoon fresh lemon juice
Salt and pepper to taste

1. Lightly steam asparagus until it is tender but still crisp. Place in a single layer on a warmed platter. Cover platter to keep asparagus warm.

2. In a small skillet, melt butter with garlic powder. Heat until butter begins to brown. Add lemon juice, salt, and pepper. Stir well and remove from heat.

3. Drizzle butter mixture over asparagus. Serve immediately.

Serves 4
Approximately 3 grams fat per serving

ASPARAGUS WITH DELICATE MUSTARD SAUCE

Lightly steamed asparagus topped with a mild, creamy mustard sauce.

1 pound fresh asparagus
3 tablespoons plus 1 teaspoon
  plain nonfat yogurt
1 tablespoon plus 1 teaspoon
  low-calorie mayonnaise
¾ teaspoon prepared mustard
Salt and pepper to taste

1. Lightly steam asparagus, until it is tender but still crisp.
2. Blend together yogurt, mayonnaise, mustard, salt, and pepper. In a small pan, heat mixture until it is warm but not boiling.
3. Spoon mixture over asparagus. Serve immediately.

Serves 4
Approximately 1.9 grams fat per serving

Variation: Broccoli with Delicate Mustard Sauce: Replace the asparagus with 4 cups broccoli flowerets.

COUNTRY BEANS

A touch of sage and nutmeg gives this green bean dish a distinctively meaty flavor.

1 28-ounce can green beans,
  drained and liquid reserved
1½ teaspoons bacon grease or
  low-calorie margarine
2 tablespoons finely chopped
  yellow onion
¼ teaspoon ground sage
⅛ teaspoon ground nutmeg
Salt and pepper to taste

1. In a heavy pot, combine liquid from green beans, bacon grease or margarine, onion, sage, nutmeg, salt, and pepper. Bring to a boil and boil until mixture is reduced to 1 cup.
2. Add beans to mixture. Cover pot tightly and simmer for 5 minutes. Remove from heat. Let stand for 10–15 minutes and serve.

Serves 4
Approximately 2 grams fat per serving

BROCCOLI WITH MILD LEMON CURRY SAUCE

Although I use this flavorful sauce on broccoli here, it's also wonderful with steamed asparagus. Try it both ways (see variation below).

3 cups broccoli flowerets
½ cup undiluted condensed cream
  of chicken soup
1 tablespoon fresh lemon juice
1 tablespoon water
¼ teaspoon curry powder
Dash salt
Paprika, if desired

1. Lightly steam broccoli, until it is tender but still crisp.

2. While broccoli is cooking, combine soup, lemon juice, water, curry powder, and salt in a small saucepan. Heat thoroughly.

3. Place broccoli on a serving platter and spoon sauce over it. Sprinkle with paprika, if desired, and serve immediately.

Serves 4
Approximately 1.7 grams fat per serving

Variation: Asparagus with Mild Lemon Curry Sauce: Substitute 1 pound fresh asparagus for the broccoli and steam lightly.

FRESH BROCCOLI AND GINGER ORIENTAL

Tossed with Oriental seasonings and topped with crispy chow mein noodles, this dish has an almost nutty flavor.

¼ cup plus 1 tablespoon water
½ teaspoon beef bouillon granules
1 tablespoon plus 1 teaspoon
  "lite" soy sauce
⅙ teaspoon (½ packet) Equal
⅛ teaspoon ground ginger
⅛ teaspoon garlic powder
4 cups broccoli flowerets
2 tablespoons crispy chow mein
  noodles

1. In a small bowl, combine water, bouillon granules, soy sauce, Equal, ginger, and garlic powder. Set aside.

2. Lightly steam broccoli, until it is tender but still crisp. Place broccoli in a serving dish and pour seasoning mixture over it. Toss well.

3. Sprinkle noodles over broccoli. Serve immediately.

Serves 4
Approximately 0.4 gram fat per serving

MOTHER'S CABBAGE

A hearty, meaty-flavored combination of cabbage, carrots, and other vegetables.

1 cup condensed beef broth
1 cup water
⅛ teaspoon ground sage
⅛ teaspoon ground nutmeg
Salt and pepper to taste
½ small head green cabbage, cut into 4 wedges
1 cup julienned carrots
½ cup chopped celery
¼ cup slivered green bell pepper
2 tablespoons chopped yellow onion
Garnish: Cider vinegar, if desired

1. In a heavy pot, combine broth, water, sage, nutmeg, salt, and pepper. Bring mixture to a boil.
2. Add cabbage, carrots, celery, bell pepper, and onion to pot. Cover and simmer for 10 minutes, turning cabbage wedges once. Remove from heat and let stand for 5 minutes.
3. A dash of vinegar can be sprinkled over the vegetables just before serving if desired.

Serves 4
Approximately 0.3 gram fat per serving

SAUTEED CABBAGE

This richly browned cabbage and onion dish is terrific for warming up a cold-weather meal.

Low-calorie cooking spray
2 teaspoons butter or margarine
¾ cup thinly sliced yellow onion
4 cups shredded green cabbage
Salt and freshly ground pepper to taste

1. Coat a large, fairly deep skillet with low-calorie cooking spray. Add butter or margarine and heat until it begins to brown. Add onion and sauté over high heat until translucent (about 2 minutes).
2. Add cabbage, salt, and pepper. Cook over medium-high heat for about 10 minutes until edges of cabbage are richly browned.

Serves 4
Approximately 2.3 grams fat per serving

CARROTS WITH BROWN SUGAR

Tender-cooked carrots take on a slightly sweet flavor when combined with brown sugar, cinnamon, and a bit of orange.

2 cups diagonally sliced carrots
2 tablespoons dark brown sugar
  (not packed)
Dash of ground cinnamon
¼ teaspoon grated orange zest

1. Lightly steam carrots, until they are tender but still crisp.
2. Toss hot carrots with brown sugar, cinnamon, and orange zest. Serve immediately.

Serves 4
Approximately 0.2 gram fat per serving

Note: Be sure to add brown sugar, cinnamon, and orange zest to carrots *just before serving.* If the dish sits for too long, the flavors of the individual ingredients will blend together and the dish will taste flat.

BUTTER-GLAZED CARROTS

Steamed fresh carrots tossed in hot, bubbly butter.

2 cups julienned carrots
1 tablespoon plus ½ teaspoon
  butter
Salt to taste
⅛ teaspoon sugar

1. Lightly steam carrots, until they are tender but still crisp.
2. In a nonstick skillet, melt butter with salt and sugar over high heat until bubbly.
3. Add steamed carrots to butter mixture and toss over high heat until a light brown glaze covers all of the carrots. Serve immediately.

Serves 4
Approximately 3.6 grams fat per serving

CAULIFLOWER AND CARROTS WITH NUTMEG

A dash of nutmeg brings out the sweetness of summer-fresh carrots and the richness of cauliflower.

2 cups cauliflower flowerets
2 cups julienned carrots
½ teaspoon ground nutmeg
3 tablespoons water
1½ teaspoons sugar
¼ teaspoon salt
2 teaspoons butter or margarine, melted

1. Preheat oven to 350°F.
2. Combine all ingredients. Toss well and place mixture in a 1½-quart casserole. Cover dish tightly and bake for 55 to 60 minutes.

Serves 4
Approximately 2.4 grams fat per serving

CAULIFLOWER IN HOT CHEESE SAUCE

Lightly steamed cauliflower smothered in a spicy, flavorful cheese sauce.

3 cups cauliflower flowerets
¼ cup skim milk
½ teaspoon flour
⅛ teaspoon paprika
Dash garlic powder
⅛ teaspoon cayenne pepper
Salt and black pepper to taste
¼ cup grated reduced-fat cheddar cheese
Paprika, if desired

1. Lightly steam cauliflower, until it is tender but still crisp.
2. In a small saucepan, mix together skim milk and flour. Cook over medium heat until sauce thickens. Remove from heat.
3. Add paprika, garlic powder, cayenne pepper, salt, and black pepper to sauce and stir thoroughly. Add cheese and stir until melted.
4. Place cauliflower on a serving platter and top with sauce. Sprinkle paprika over the dish, if desired, and serve immediately.

Serves 4
Approximately 1.4 grams fat per serving

ORIENTAL CELERY

Seasoned celery and onion in a Chinese-style sauce.

1 cup canned or homemade
  chicken broth
3 cups diagonally sliced celery
1 cup sliced yellow onion
2 teaspoons cornstarch
1 teaspoon "lite" soy sauce
Dash garlic powder
Salt and pepper to taste

1. In a nonstick skillet, bring chicken broth to a boil. Add celery and onion. Cover and simmer until vegetables are tender but still crisp (3 to 4 minutes).

2. In a small bowl, combine cornstarch, soy sauce, garlic powder, salt, and pepper. Add mixture to vegetables. Stir until sauce thickens. Remove from heat and serve immediately.

Serves 4
Approximately 0.1 gram fat per serving

Variation: French Celery: Omit the soy sauce and add about 2 tablespoons white wine.

GREEN BEANS WITH HERBED "BUTTER"

This is a light, elegant vegetable dish. It's a wonderful accompaniment to almost any main course.

2 tablespoons plus 2 teaspoons
   low-calorie margarine
1 teaspoon fresh lemon juice
¼ teaspoon dried basil leaves
¼ teaspoon dried parsley flakes
½ teaspoon dried dill
Dash garlic powder
Dash salt
Low-calorie cooking spray
3 tablespoons finely chopped
   yellow onion
1 pound fresh green beans,
   trimmed, cleaned, and lightly
   steamed
Salt and pepper to taste

1. In a small bowl, combine margarine, lemon juice, basil, parsley, dill, garlic powder, and a dash of salt. Mix together and refrigerate for 20 minutes.

2. Coat a large skillet with low-calorie cooking spray. Heat skillet. Add onion and sauté over medium heat until lightly browned (about 1 minute).

3. Add green beans and salt and pepper to taste. Cover skillet and cook over medium heat for 2 to 3 minutes. Remove from heat.

4. Transfer vegetables to four individual serving plates. Spoon 2 teaspoons herbed margarine onto each serving.

Serves 4
Approximately 3.2 grams fat per serving

GREEN BEANS ITALIAN STYLE

The fennel seed in this distinctive dish makes for a deliciously flavored vegetable combination.

½ teaspoon olive oil
½ cup thinly sliced green bell
   pepper
1 small yellow onion, sliced thin
½ pound fresh green beans, cut
   into bite-sized pieces
1 cup undrained chopped canned
   tomatoes
¼ cup water
1 teaspoon fresh lemon juice
¼ teaspoon garlic salt
⅛ teaspoon fennel seed
⅛ teaspoon freshly ground pepper
¼ teaspoon dried basil leaves
2 teaspoons freshly grated
   Parmesan cheese

1. Heat olive oil in a large, heavy skillet. Add bell pepper and onion and sauté over medium-high heat until the vegetables are tender (2 to 3 minutes).

2. Add green beans, tomatoes, water, lemon juice, garlic salt, fennel seed, pepper, and basil. Reduce heat to low and cover the skillet. Cook for 20 minutes or until green beans are tender.

3. Just before serving, sprinkle cheese over vegetables.

Serves 4
Approximately 0.9 gram fat per serving

MUSHROOMS IN BEEF BURGUNDY SAUCE

A rich brown sauce, enlivened by a hint of wine, makes these mushrooms a hearty treat.

Low-calorie cooking spray
1 teaspoon butter or margarine
1 pound fresh mushrooms
⅛ teaspoon garlic powder
Salt and pepper to taste
1 cup canned or homemade beef
   broth
2 tablespoons burgundy
1 tablespoon cornstarch
⅛ teaspoon sugar
Dash Worcestershire sauce

1. Coat a nonstick skillet with low-calorie cooking spray. Add butter or margarine and heat until hot and bubbly. Add mushrooms, garlic powder, salt, and pepper and sauté over medium-high heat for 2 to 3 minutes.

2. In a small bowl, combine broth, wine, cornstarch, sugar, and Worcestershire sauce. Blend thoroughly and pour mixture over mushrooms. Simmer for 5 minutes. Serve in individual ramekins or small bowls.

Serves 4
Approximately 1.1 grams fat per serving

BROILED MUSHROOMS WITH HERBED BUTTER

This side dish is a flavorful addition to almost any entree. I especially like it with Pan-Fried Steak with Red Wine Sauce (see Index).

2 tablespoons plus 1 teaspoon low-calorie margarine
½ teaspoon dried basil leaves
1 teaspoon fresh lemon juice
½ teaspoon dried parsley flakes
¼ teaspoon dried tarragon or dried dill
1 pound fresh mushrooms, quartered
1 tablespoon Worcestershire sauce
¼ teaspoon garlic powder
¼ teaspoon salt
⅛ teaspoon freshly ground black pepper

1. In a small bowl, combine butter, basil, lemon juice, parsley, and tarragon or dill. Let stand for 20 minutes.
2. In a large bowl, combine mushrooms, Worcestershire sauce, garlic powder, salt, and pepper. Toss gently but thoroughly.
3. Place mushroom mixture on a cookie sheet and broil, 5 inches from heat source, until mushrooms are tender (5 to 6 minutes). Transfer mushroom mixture to four individual ramekins or small bowls. Top each serving with 1½ teaspoons herbed butter.

Serves 4
Approximately 3.6 grams fat per serving

OVEN-FRIED MUSHROOMS AND ZUCCHINI

Breaded and seasoned with Italian flavorings, this vegetable dish is very popular with french fry lovers.

1½ slices "diet" bread, toasted and grated
¼ teaspoon dried basil leaves
⅛ teaspoon dried oregano leaves
⅛ teaspoon garlic powder
3 tablespoons freshly grated Romano cheese
2 cups quartered fresh mushrooms
1 small zucchini, cut into julienne strips
⅓ cup oil-free Italian dressing
Garnish: Lemon wedges

1. Preheat oven to 475°F.
2. Combine bread crumbs, basil, oregano, garlic powder, and cheese.
3. Dip mushrooms and zucchini in salad dressing. Roll in bread crumb mixture.
4. Place vegetables in a single layer on a nonstick cookie sheet. Bake for 5 minutes. Carefully turn vegetables and bake for an additional 3 to 4 minutes. Garnish with lemon wedges, and serve immediately.

Serves 4
Approximately 1.2 grams fat per serving

STEWED OKRA AND TOMATOES

A hearty combination of okra, bell pepper, onion, and tomato simmered in flavorful herbs.

Low-calorie cooking spray
1 teaspoon butter or margarine
⅔ cup chopped yellow onion
½ cup chopped green bell pepper
1½ cups sliced fresh okra
2 medium-sized tomatoes, quartered
1 tablespoon chopped fresh parsley
½ teaspoon salt
⅛ teaspoon garlic powder
⅛ teaspoon sugar
⅛ teaspoon pepper
1 bay leaf

1. Coat a large skillet with low-calorie cooking spray. Melt butter or margarine in the skillet. Add onion and bell pepper and sauté over medium-high heat until vegetables are tender (2 to 3 minutes).

2. Add okra, tomatoes, parsley, salt, garlic powder, sugar, pepper, and bay leaf to skillet. Reduce heat to medium, cover, and cook for 7 minutes, stirring occasionally. Remove from heat and let stand for 5 minutes. Remove bay leaf before serving.

Serves 4
Approximately 1.4 grams fat per serving

OVEN-FRIED OKRA

Fresh, delicious okra baked in a crunchy Cajun breading.

¾ pound fresh okra
1½ slices "diet" bread, toasted and grated
¼ teaspoon Cajun seasoning
⅓ cup oil-free Italian dressing
Low-calorie cooking spray

1. Preheat oven to 350°F.
2. Cut okra into ½-inch-thick slices.
3. Mix together bread crumbs and Cajun seasoning. Dip okra slices in salad dressing and roll in bread crumb mixture.

4. Liberally coat a nonstick cookie sheet with low-calorie cooking spray. Place okra on the cookie sheet and bake for 15 minutes. Turn okra over and bake for another 15 minutes. Serve immediately.

Serves 4
Approximately 0.2 gram fat per serving

THE GRILLED ONION

Foil-wrapped seasoned onions are a delicious, easy-to-make accompaniment to any main course.

4 medium-sized yellow onions,
   peeled and trimmed
2 teaspoons low-calorie margarine
Seasoned salt to taste
Freshly ground pepper to taste

1. Preheat oven to 350°F.
2. Score each onion by cutting a ½-inch-deep X into the top. Place each onion on a square of aluminum foil (foil should be large enough to enclose onion). Put ½ teaspoon margarine on top of each onion. Sprinkle each with desired amount of seasoned salt and pepper.
3. Seal foil tightly around onions and bake for 35 to 40 minutes.

Serves 4
Approximately 0.9 gram fat per serving

Note: These can also be prepared on the grill. Simply seal the foil tightly around onions and grill over ashen coals for 40 to 45 minutes or until cooked.

BAKED CLOVED ONIONS

Delicately spiced, these sweet baked onions are a tempting side dish on cold nights.

4 medium-sized yellow onions,
   peeled and trimmed
32 cloves
¼ cup "lite" soy sauce
½ teaspoon sugar
¼ teaspoon garlic powder
¼ teaspoon ground ginger
Freshly ground pepper to taste

1. Preheat oven to 350°F.
2. Score each onion by cutting a ½-inch-deep X into the top. Spear each onion with eight cloves.
3. Mix together soy sauce, sugar, garlic powder, and ginger. Spoon 1 tablespoon of the mixture over each onion.
4. Place in 8″ × 12″ baking dish and bake, uncovered, for 35 to 45 minutes or until tender, basting frequently.
5. Serve onions in foil, with the corners of the foil turned back, to keep the juices in. Sprinkle each onion with pepper just before serving.

Serves 4
Approximately 0.1 gram fat per serving

PEAS AND WATER CHESTNUTS

An eye-catching blend of delicate vegetables, this side dish dresses up any main course.

1⅓ cups frozen peas with pearl
   onions
1 2-ounce can mushroom slices,
   well-drained
½ cup drained sliced water
   chestnuts
2 tablespoons finely chopped red
   bell pepper
Salt and pepper to taste
⅓ teaspoon (1 packet) Equal, if
   desired

Combine all ingredients. Steam lightly, until peas have cooked but are still crisp. Remove from heat and serve.

Serves 4
Approximately 0.2 gram fat per serving

ALL-AMERICAN OVEN FRIES

Yes, you can have fries and still diet! The thinner the fries, the better they taste.

2 small potatoes (11 ounces total),
   peeled if desired
Low-calorie cooking spray
Salt and pepper to taste

1. Preheat oven to 375°F.
2. Cut potatoes into paper-thin slices resembling potato chips. (This is easiest to do in a food processor fitted with the slicing disk.)
3. Liberally coat two nonstick cookie sheets with low-calorie cooking spray. Arrange potatoes in one layer on the cookie sheets. Sprinkle with salt and pepper and bake for 15 minutes. Turn potatoes over and bake for an additional 10 to 12 minutes.

Serves 4
Approximately 0.1 gram fat per serving

Note: For crunchy *and* spicy fries, sprinkle potatoes with Cajun seasoning before baking.

Variation: Dilled Oven Fries: Prepare the potatoes as directed, but toss them with 1 tablespoon plus 1 teaspoon fresh lemon juice and 1 teaspoon dried dill before baking.

CREAMED SPINACH

Rich and elegant, this makes a perfect vegetable for holiday meals. No one will believe that this dish is as low in calories as it is.

1 10-ounce package frozen chopped spinach, cooked according to directions on package
Low-calorie cooking spray
¼ cup low-fat (1 percent fat) cottage cheese
3 tablespoons skim milk
¼ cup freshly grated Parmesan cheese
Dash ground nutmeg
Salt and pepper to taste
¼ teaspoon onion powder, if desired

1. Preheat oven to 350°F.
2. In a colander, squeeze and discard excess liquid from spinach.
3. Lightly coat a casserole dish with low-calorie cooking spray. Place spinach in dish.
4. Using a blender or a food processor fitted with the steel blade, blend together cottage cheese and skim milk until smooth. Add mixture to spinach. Stir in Parmesan cheese, nutmeg, salt, pepper, and onion powder if desired. Bake uncovered for 10 minutes or until thoroughly heated.

Serves 4
Approximately 1.5 grams fat per serving

SUMMER SQUASH CASSEROLE

A hearty dish of country vegetables baked in cheese and bread crumbs.

¾ pound yellow squash, sliced

¼ cup chopped scallion

¼ cup grated carrot

2 tablespoons finely chopped red bell pepper

¼ cup grated reduced-fat cheddar cheese

1 medium-sized egg white, well beaten

¼ teaspoon seasoned salt

⅛ teaspoon pepper

½ slice "diet" bread, toasted and grated

1 tablespoon chopped fresh parsley

⅛ teaspoon paprika

1. Preheat oven to 350°F.

2. Steam squash until tender but still crisp.

3. In a mixing bowl, combine squash, scallion, carrot, red bell pepper, cheese, egg white, seasoned salt, and pepper. Stir gently. Spoon into a 6″ x 10″ baking dish.

4. Combine bread crumbs, parsley, and paprika. Mix well and sprinkle over squash mixture. Bake for 20 minutes or until thoroughly heated.

Serves 4
Approximately 1.4 grams fat per serving

Note: For convenience, bread crumbs may be made up in a large quantity and frozen in a zip-lock freezer bag. Keep in mind that 1 slice "diet" bread equals ¼ cup bread crumbs. One-half slice "diet" bread equals 2 tablespoons bread crumbs.

SQUASH MEDLEY

A perfect dish for summer, when the summer squash and zucchini crops bloom forth in typical abundance.

Low-calorie cooking spray
¾ cup sliced yellow onion
1 small zucchini, sliced thin
2 medium yellow squash, sliced thin
1 cup undrained canned tomatoes
1 teaspoon sugar
¾ teaspoon salt
½ teaspoon dried basil leaves
Dash pepper

1. Lightly coat a nonstick skillet with low-calorie cooking spray. Heat skillet. Add onion and sauté over high heat until lightly browned (about 2 minutes).
2. Reduce heat to low. Add zucchini, yellow squash, tomatoes, sugar, salt, basil, and pepper to onions. Cover pan and simmer for 25 minutes.

Serves 4
Approximately 0.1 gram fat per serving

BAKED SQUASH PARMESAN

Here's another tasty way to serve this abundantly available summer vegetable.

4 medium-sized yellow squash
2 teaspoons low-calorie margarine, melted
2 tablespoons finely chopped scallion
¼ cup freshly grated Parmesan cheese
Salt and pepper to taste

1. Preheat oven to 350°F.
2. Cut each squash in half lengthwise. Place on a cookie sheet.
3. Drizzle ½ teaspoon melted margarine over each squash half. Sprinkle scallion evenly over squash halves. Top each half with Parmesan cheese and add salt and pepper to taste.
4. Bake for 25 to 30 minutes or until tender.

Serves 4
Approximately 2.4 grams fat per serving

A FINELY BROILED TOMATO

This is a quick, easy way to prepare a sophisticated-looking side dish.

2 large tomatoes, halved crosswise
¼ cup oil-free Italian dressing
½ slice "diet" bread, toasted and grated
3 tablespoons freshly grated Parmesan cheese
2 tablespoons chopped fresh parsley
Salt and pepper to taste

1. Preheat the broiler.
2. Place tomato halves on a cookie sheet. Spoon 1 tablespoon salad dressing over each half.
3. Combine bread crumbs and cheese. Sprinkle evenly over tomato halves. Top each with parsley and add salt and pepper to taste. Broil tomatoes, 5 inches from heat source, for 3 minutes. Turn off broiler and leave tomatoes in for 3 more minutes.

Serves 4
Approximately 1.1 grams fat per serving

BROILED TOMATOES DIJON

Broiled fresh tomatoes highlighted with spicy Dijon mustard, savory bread crumbs, cheese, and herbs.

4 medium-sized tomatoes, halved crosswise
2 teaspoons Dijon mustard
½ slice "diet" bread, toasted and grated
2 tablespoons freshly grated Parmesan cheese
1 teaspoon dried parsley flakes
½ teaspoon dried basil leaves
¼ teaspoon salt
⅛ teaspoon cayenne pepper

1. Preheat the broiler.
2. Place tomato halves on a cookie sheet. Brush each tomato half with ¼ teaspoon mustard. Mix together bread crumbs, cheese, parsley, basil, salt, and cayenne pepper and sprinkle mixture over tomato halves.
3. Broil tomatoes, 5 inches from the heat source, for 3 minutes. Turn off broiler and leave tomatoes in for 3 more minutes.

Serves 4
Approximately 0.8 gram fat per serving

TOMATO CASSEROLE

This dish is very easy and quick to prepare and gives a vibrant touch of color to any meal.

2 16-ounce cans quartered drained tomatoes
2 tablespoons finely chopped yellow onion
1 teaspoon low-calorie margarine, melted
Salt and pepper to taste
1 slice "diet" bread, toasted and grated
¼ teaspoon dried oregano leaves
¼ teaspoon dried basil leaves
⅛ teaspoon seasoned salt
⅛ teaspoon garlic powder
Freshly ground pepper, if desired

1. Preheat oven to 350°F.
2. Cut tomatoes into large chunks. Place in a 9-inch square casserole dish. Add onion.
3. Drizzle melted margarine over vegetables. Add salt and pepper to taste and toss gently. Bake for 20 minutes. Remove dish from oven and reset oven to broil.
4. Combine bread crumbs, oregano, basil, seasoned salt, and garlic powder. Mix well and sprinkle over baked vegetables. Broil, 5 inches from heat source, for 1 to 2 minutes or until the bread crumbs are lightly browned.
5. Just before serving, top dish with freshly ground pepper if desired.

Serves 4
Approximately 0.5 gram fat per serving

BAKED TOMATOES WITH CHEESE

A light side dish with more than a touch of sophisticated flair. No one will believe how truly easy it is to prepare.

Low-calorie cooking spray
4 large tomatoes, cut into
  ¾-inch-thick slices
1 tablespoon plus 1½ teaspoons
  oil-free Italian dressing
8 small pitted black olives, sliced
1 2-ounce can mushrooms,
  well-drained and chopped
¼ cup finely grated mozzarella
  cheese
1 tablespoon Italian-seasoned
  bread crumbs
1 tablespoon chopped fresh
  parsley
½ teaspoon dried oregano leaves

1. Preheat oven to 350°F.
2. Coat a nonstick cookie sheet with low-calorie cooking spray. Arrange tomato slices on cookie sheet and drizzle salad dressing over them.
3. Top tomatoes with olives and mushrooms, then cheese.
4. Combine bread crumbs, parsley, and oregano and sprinkle on top of cheese.
5. Bake for 8 to 10 minutes or until cheese has melted.

Serves 4
Approximately 3.3 grams fat per serving

COUNTRY TURNIPS

This recipe combines fresh and frozen turnips for an easy-to-make, country-rich side dish.

½ bacon strip
1 cup water
1 10-ounce package frozen turnips
1 medium-sized fresh turnip root,
  cut into bite-sized pieces
½ teaspoon sugar
½ teaspoon salt

1. In a heavy skillet, cook bacon over medium-high heat until well done but not burned. Remove bacon from skillet. Crumble and place back in pot with bacon grease.
2. Add water to bacon. Bring mixture to a boil.
3. Add frozen and fresh turnips, sugar, and salt. Return mixture to a full boil, then reduce heat and cover skillet. Simmer for 30 minutes or until fresh turnip is tender.
4. Remove from heat and let stand for 15 to 20 minutes.

Serves 4
Approximately 2.1 grams fat per serving

ZUCCHINI TOSS

Fresh zucchini, onions, and herbs, sautéed and tossed with Parmesan cheese.

Low-calorie cooking spray
1 teaspoon olive oil
2½ cups julienned zucchini
1 tablespoon minced onion
1 teaspoon dried oregano leaves
2 tablespoons plus 2 teaspoons
  freshly grated Parmesan cheese

1. Preheat the broiler.
2. Coat a nonstick skillet with low-calorie cooking spray. Heat olive oil in the skillet. Add zucchini, onion, and oregano. Cover skillet and cook over medium-high heat for 2 minutes. Uncover and cook for 2 minutes more, stirring occasionally, until vegetables are lightly browned and tender. Remove from heat.
3. Toss cheese into vegetables. Place mixture in an ovenproof dish and broil, 2–3 inches from heat source, for 1 minute. Serve immediately.

Serves 4
Approximately 2.4 grams fat per serving

BAKED MELANGE

Full-bodied, butter- and herb-baked vegetables. This is delicious with grilled meats.

Low-calorie cooking spray
2 medium-sized tomatoes, each
  cut into 8 pieces
1 large green bell pepper, chopped
  into bite-sized pieces
½ medium-sized yellow onion, cut
  into strips
½ cup thinly sliced yellow squash
1 tablespoon chopped fresh
  parsley
½ teaspoon dried basil leaves
¼ teaspoon salt
⅛ teaspoon pepper
¼ teaspoon sugar
⅛ teaspoon garlic powder
1 tablespoon plus 1 teaspoon
  low-calorie margarine, melted

1. Preheat oven to 350°F.
2. Coat a 1½-quart casserole dish with low-calorie cooking spray. Place tomatoes, bell pepper, onion, and squash in dish.
3. Mix together parsley, basil, salt, pepper, sugar, and garlic powder. Sprinkle seasoning mixture evenly over vegetables. Drizzle melted margarine over the casserole, then toss well.
4. Tightly cover dish and bake for 1 hour or until vegetables are tender, stirring once after 30 minutes.

Serves 4
Approximately 1.4 grams fat per serving

PLAIN AND SIMPLE 50-CALORIE VEGETABLE DISHES

When you don't have the time (or the energy) to create a more elaborate vegetable dish, these quick and easy alternatives can save the meal—and your diet. All of these vegetables can be seasoned with your choice of herbs, spices, lemon juice, or butter-substitute seasonings.

Asparagus: 9 fresh spears equal one 50-calorie serving. Approximately 0.3 gram fat per serving.

Beets: 2 medium-sized fresh or ¾ cup canned equals one 50-calorie serving. Approximately 0.2 gram fat per serving.

Broccoli: 1½ stalks fresh or 1⅓ cups frozen equal one 50-calorie serving. Approximately 0.5 gram fat per serving.

Brussels Sprouts: 9 medium-sized fresh or 1 cup frozen equals one 50-calorie serving. Approximately 0.4 gram fat per serving.

Cabbage: 2 cups shredded equal one 50-calorie serving. Approximately 0.4 gram fat per serving.

Carrots: 2½ small fresh or 1 cup frozen equals one 50-calorie serving. Approximately 0.3 gram fat per serving.

Cauliflower: 2 cups fresh or 1⅓ cups frozen equal one 50-calorie serving. Approximately 0.4 gram fat per serving.

Corn: ½ cup equals one 50-calorie serving. Approximately 0.5 gram fat per serving.

Eggplant: 1 cup diced equals one 50-calorie serving. Approximately 0.4 gram fat per serving.

Green Beans: 1½ cups equal one 50-calorie serving. Approximately 0.3 gram fat per serving.

Green Bell Pepper: 2 large-sized equal one 50-calorie serving. Approximately 0.4 gram fat per serving.

Mixed Vegetables: ½ cup frozen equals one 50-calorie serving. Approximately 0.2 gram fat per serving.

Mushrooms: 2 cups fresh or 1 cup drained, canned equals one 50-calorie serving. Approximately 0.6 gram fat per serving.

Okra: 11 fresh pods or 1 cup frozen equals one 50-calorie serving. Approximately 0.4 gram fat per serving.

Onions: 1 small (about 2½ inches in diameter) fresh or 1 cup frozen equals one 50-calorie serving. Approximately 0.2 gram fat per serving.

Potatoes: 1 small (about 2½ ounces) equals one 50-calorie serving. Approximately 0.1 gram fat per serving.

Rutabagas: ¾ cup equals one 50-calorie serving. Approximately 0.1 gram fat per serving.

Spinach: 1⅓ cups frozen equal one 50-calorie serving. Approximately 0.5 gram fat per serving.

Squash: 1½ cups fresh equal one 50-calorie serving. Approximately 0.3 gram fat per serving.

Tomatoes: 1 large fresh or 1¼ cups canned equal one 50-calorie serving. Approximately 0.4 gram fat per serving.

Turnips: 2½ cups fresh or 1½ cups canned equal one 50-calorie serving. Approximately 0.6 gram fat per serving.

Water Chestnuts: 10 whole equal one 50-calorie serving. Approximately 0.3 gram fat per serving.

7
❧ DESSERTS ❧

RHUBARB-PINEAPPLE COMPOTE

A beautiful chilled dessert of fresh rhubarb and pineapple stewed in brown sugar and cinnamon.

12 ounces fresh rhubarb, cut into
   1-inch pieces
½ teaspoon vanilla extract
3 tablespoons water
¼ cup dark brown sugar (not
   packed)
⅛ teaspoon baking soda
½ teaspoon ground cinnamon
¾ cup finely chopped fresh
   pineapple
⅔ teaspoon (2 packets) Equal, if
   desired

Combine all ingredients in a saucepan. Tightly cover pan and simmer mixture until fruit is tender yet still crisp (about 10 minutes). Chill and serve.

Serves 5
Approximately 0.1 gram fat per serving

TROPICAL LEMON CREAM SQUARES

Rich, creamy lemon squares with a not-so-subtle hint of fresh, ripe banana.

1 3-ounce package sugar-free
   lemon gelatin
1 cup boiling water
¾ cup cold water
1 cup plain nonfat yogurt
½ cup well-mashed very ripe
   banana
½ teaspoon vanilla extract

1. Combine gelatin and boiling water. Stir until gelatin is dissolved, then add cold water. Add yogurt, banana, and vanilla extract and, using a whisk, blend thoroughly.
2. Pour into an 8-inch square pan. Chill until set (about 2 hours). Cut into squares and serve immediately.

Serves 4
Approximately 0.1 gram fat per serving

Variation: Pineapple Cream Squares: Substitute ½ cup drained canned crushed pineapple in its own juice for the banana.

GINGERED FRUIT IN PLUM WINE

Fresh pineapple and strawberries marinated in a sweet plum wine, with a hint of ginger as well.

¾ cup diced fresh pineapple
1¼ cups halved fresh strawberries
¼ cup plum wine
⅛ teaspoon ground ginger

Combine all ingredients in a decorative glass serving bowl. Seal bowl with plastic wrap and chill for 4 hours, stirring frequently.

Serves 4
Approximately 0.4 gram fat per serving

PEACHES AND CREAM WITH NUTMEG

These sugar-tossed fresh peaches with a heavenly whipped topping and a dash of nutmeg are particularly nice to serve after a grilled main course.

2 cups sliced fresh peaches
1 teaspoon sugar
½ cup prepared Dream Whip topping
¼ teaspoon ground nutmeg

1. In a mixing bowl, toss peaches with sugar. Let stand at room temperature for 30 minutes.
2. Place ½ cup peaches on each of four dessert dishes. Refrigerate until serving time.
3. Just before serving, top each with 2 tablespoons whipped topping. Sprinkle with nutmeg and serve.

Serves 4
Approximately 0.9 gram fat per serving

STRAWBERRIES IN VANILLA CREAM

To get the full flavor and sweetness from the strawberries, let them stand at room temperature overnight before making this dish.

2 cups halved fresh strawberries
½ teaspoon powdered sugar
½ cup low-fat vanilla yogurt

1. Place ½ cup strawberries in each of four champagne glasses or decorative serving bowls.
2. Combine powdered sugar and yogurt. Mix well and spoon 2 tablespoons over each serving.

Serves 4
Approximately 0.8 gram fat per serving

FROZEN SUGAR-COATED GRAPES

An incredibly easy-to-make, yet colorful and refreshing, low-calorie dessert.

1 cup seedless green grapes
¾ cup seedless red grapes
1½ teaspoons sugar

1. Rinse grapes. Shake off excess water (do not blot dry).

2. Place grapes in one layer on a cookie sheet. Sprinkle with sugar and freeze for 1 hour.

3. Divide grapes evenly among four champagne glasses or decorative bowls (slightly less than ½ cup in each). Let stand for 5 minutes and serve.

Serves 4
Approximately 0.6 gram fat per serving

BAKED PEARS IN ORANGE-RAISIN SAUCE

This dessert is especially nice to serve in the chilly fall and winter months—pears baked in a citrus sauce and seasoned with cinnamon and allspice.

2 fresh pears, peeled
¼ cup of fresh orange juice
¼ cup water
1 tablespoon raisins
1 teaspoon cornstarch
¼ teaspoon grated orange zest
⅛ teaspoon ground cinnamon
Dash ground allspice

1. Preheat oven to 425°F.

2. Cut pears in half lengthwise and core them. Pierce cut sides of each half with a fork in several places. Arrange, cut side up, in an 8-inch square baking dish.

3. Cut raisins in half and combine all remaining ingredients in a small saucepan. Bring to a boil and boil for 1 minute. Pour sauce over pears.

4. Cover dish with foil and bake for 45 minutes or until pears are tender. Place one half in each of four dessert bowls and spoon 2 tablespoons sauce over each serving.

Serves 4
Approximately 0.2 gram fat per serving

CHOCOLATE CREPES WITH STRAWBERRIES

Rich chocolate crepes filled with sweetened fresh strawberries, rolled, and dusted with powdered sugar.

Crepes
⅔ cup skim milk
½ cup flour
1 tablespoon unsweetened cocoa
   powder
⅓ cup water
⅔ teaspoon (2 packets) Equal
1 teaspoon vanilla extract
1 medium-sized egg white at room
   temperature
¼ teaspoon cream of tartar
Low-calorie cooking spray

Filling
1⅓ cups quartered strawberries
⅔ teaspoon (2 packets) Equal

Topping
2 teaspoons powdered sugar

To Make Crepes:
   1. In a mixing bowl, combine skim milk, flour, cocoa, water, Equal, and vanilla extract. Beat until smooth.
   2. In a separate bowl, place egg white and cream of tartar. Beat until mixture forms stiff peaks. Fold into batter. Cover bowl and refrigerate for 2 hours.
   3. Coat a nonstick skillet with low-calorie cooking spray and place over medium-high heat. When skillet is hot, pour 2 tablespoons batter into pan. Quickly tilt the pan in a circular motion to spread batter into a thin film. Cook for 1 minute. To test for doneness, lift the edges of the crepe. When the edges lift easily without sticking, turn crepe over and cook for 45 seconds more.
   4. Place crepes on a towel to cool. Stack between layers of wax paper to prevent sticking and freeze whatever quantity is not needed at the time. For this recipe, you will need four crepes. Leftover crepes may be frozen for up to 2 weeks. To use, simply thaw.

Makes 14 crepes

To Make Filling and Fill Crepes:
   1. Combine strawberries with Equal and let stand for 30 minutes.
   2. Preheat oven to 350°F.
   3. Just before serving time, fill each of the four crepes with equal amounts of strawberries (slightly over ¼ cup). Roll crepes up and place in a baking dish. Bake for 5 minutes. Remove from oven, dust crepes with powdered sugar, and serve immediately.

Serves 4
Approximately 0.4 gram fat per serving

LIGHT CREPES WITH APPLES AND CINNAMON SUGAR

Light crepes filled with stewed apples and rich spices, rolled, and topped with cinnamon sugar.

Crepes
⅔ cup skim milk
½ cup flour
⅓ cup water
⅔ teaspoon (2 packets) Equal
1 teaspoon vanilla extract
1 medium-sized egg white at room temperature
¼ teaspoon cream of tartar
Low-calorie cooking spray

Filling
1 cup peeled and thinly sliced Red Delicious apple
4 tablespoons water
1 tablespoon plus 2 teaspoons apple juice concentrate
1½ teaspoons dark brown sugar (not packed)
½ teaspoon apple pie spice
¼ teaspoon vanilla extract
Dash salt
½ teaspoon arrowroot
⅓ teaspoon (1 packet) Equal

Topping
1 teaspoon sugar
⅛ teaspoon ground cinnamon

To Make Crepes:
1. In a mixing bowl, combine skim milk, flour, water, Equal, and vanilla extract. Beat until smooth.
2. In a separate bowl, place egg white and cream of tartar. Beat until mixture forms stiff peaks. Fold into batter. Cover bowl and refrigerate for 2 hours.
3. Coat a nonstick pan with low-calorie cooking spray and place over medium-high heat. When pan is hot, pour 2 tablespoons batter into pan. Quickly tilt the pan in a circular motion to spread batter into a thin film. Cook for 1 minute. When the edges lift easily without sticking, turn crepe over and cook for 45 seconds more.
4. Place crepes on a towel to cool. Stack between layers of wax paper to prevent sticking and freeze whatever quantity is not needed at the time. For this recipe, you will need four crepes. Leftover crepes may be frozen for up to 2 weeks. To use, simply thaw.

Makes 14 crepes

To Make Filling and Fill Crepes:
1. Preheat oven to 350°F.
2. Place apple, 2 tablespoons of the water, apple juice, brown sugar, apple pie spice, vanilla extract, and salt in a saucepan. Bring to a boil, then simmer, covered, for 10 to 12 minutes or until apple is tender. Combine remaining water, arrowroot, and Equal in a separate bowl. Mix together and add to apple mixture. Place over medium-high heat and cook until bubbly and slightly thickened (about 2 minutes).
3. Place 2 tablespoons apple mixture onto each crepe. Roll them up and place in a baking dish. Combine sugar and cinnamon. Sprinkle ¼ teaspoon of the mixture over each crepe and bake for 5 minutes. Serve immediately.

Serves 4
Approximately 2 grams fat per serving

BLUEBERRIES AND WINE

Slightly tart blueberries marinated in white wine and fresh lime juice.

2 cups fresh blueberries
½ cup grape diet soda
¼ cup dry white wine
1½ teaspoons fresh lime juice
Garnish: Lime slices

1. Combine all ingredients except garnish in a mixing bowl. Refrigerate for 20 minutes.
2. Place about ½ cup of the mixture in each of four dessert dishes. Garnish with lime slices and serve.

Serves 4
Approximately 0.4 gram fat per serving

CHERRIES IN CHAMPAGNE

Nothing could be simpler, yet more festive, than this elegant dessert.

1¾ cups halved and pitted fresh
   dark sweet cherries
¼ cup champagne

1. Place cherries in a mixing bowl. Pour in champagne and refrigerate for 25 minutes, stirring occasionally.
2. Place cherries in a single layer on a cookie sheet and freeze for 2 hours. Remove from freezer and place ½ cup cherries in each of four champagne glasses. Let stand for 5 minutes and serve.

Serves 4.
Approximately 0.2 gram fat per serving

BAKED APPLES WITH WHIPPED CREAM

Oven-baked hot spicy apples, garnished with whipped topping and a dash of nutmeg.

2 medium-sized halved and cored
  apples
⅔ teaspoon (2 packets) Equal
½ teaspoon apple pie spice
¼ cup prepared Dream Whip
  topping
Ground nutmeg to taste

1. Preheat oven to 350°F.
2. Place apple halves, skin side down, in a 9-inch square baking dish. In a separate bowl, combine Equal and pie spice. Sprinkle over apples and bake, uncovered, for 30 minutes.
3. Spoon 1 tablespoon whipped topping over each apple half and sprinkle each lightly with nutmeg. Serve immediately.

Serves 4
Approximately 0.6 gram fat per serving

MY WILLIE'S APPLES

Fresh sweet apple, tossed in sugar and cinnamon and baked to produce its own rich sauce. When using apples for this and any other dessert, it's important to select the sweetest ones you can find.

2 medium-sized apples, cut into
  bite-sized pieces
2 teaspoons sugar
¼ teaspoon ground cinnamon

1. Preheat oven to 350°F.
2. Combine all ingredients in a 1-quart casserole dish. Toss well and cover the dish with foil (if the dish has a lid, use that as well). Bake for 30 to 35 minutes.
3. Remove from oven and toss well. Place equal amounts (about ½ cup) of apple mixture into four individual dessert bowls and spoon juices over each. Serve immediately.

Serves 4
Approximately 0.2 gram fat per serving

STRAWBERRY SORBET

A *light, refreshing strawberry and orange freeze.*

1½ cups fresh strawberries
¾ cup fresh orange juice
1 medium-sized egg white at room temperature
⅔ teaspoon (2 packets) Equal

1. Place strawberries and orange juice in a blender or food processor fitted with the steel blade. Blend thoroughly and set aside.
2. In a small bowl, beat egg white until foamy. Add Equal and beat until mixture forms stiff peaks. Gently but thoroughly fold egg white mixture into strawberry puree.
3. Pour mixture into a 9-inch square glass dish. Cover with plastic wrap and freeze for 3 hours, stirring mixture once each hour.

Serves 4
Approximately 0.4 gram fat per serving

STRAWBERRIES WITH MINTED CHOCOLATE

This is a very pretty dish—quite nice to serve when an elegant dessert is called for.

2 cups halved fresh strawberries
1 tablespoon plus 2 teaspoons powdered sugar
1½ teaspoons unsweetened cocoa powder
1½ teaspoons skim milk
⅛ teaspoon peppermint extract

1. Arrange ½ cup strawberries on each of four dessert plates.
2. In a mixing bowl, combine sugar, cocoa, skim milk, and peppermint extract. Let stand for 5 to 10 minutes.
3. Just before serving, slowly drizzle 1 teaspoon of the chocolate mixture over each serving. Serve immediately.

Serves 4
Approximately 0.1 gram fat per serving

CHOCOLATE MERINGUE PUFFS

A crunchy, almond-flavored chocolate puff.

2 medium-sized egg whites at
  room temperature
¼ teaspoon cream of tartar
⅛ teaspoon salt
¼ teaspoon vanilla extract
¼ teaspoon almond extract
3 tablespoons plus 2 teaspoons
  sugar
1½ teaspoons unsweetened cocoa
  powder

1. Preheat oven to 275°F.
2. In a small bowl, beat egg whites at high speed until foamy. Add cream of tartar, salt, and vanilla and almond extracts and beat until soft peaks form. In a separate bowl, mix together sugar and cocoa. Add to egg mixture, 1 tablespoon at a time, beating constantly until stiff peaks form.
3. Line a baking sheet with aluminum foil. Spoon 8 uniformly sized mounds of mixture onto sheet. Bake for 1 hour. Turn off the oven but leave meringue puffs in the oven, with the door closed, for 2 hours more. Remove from oven when meringues are dry to finish cooling. Serve.

Serves 4
Approximately 0.1 gram fat per serving

DROPPED STRAWBERRIES

A light, refreshing dessert, full of delicious strawberries-and-cream flavor.

1 3-ounce package sugar-free
  strawberry gelatin
1 cup boiling water
10 ice cubes
¾ cup plain nonfat yogurt
¾ cup thinly sliced fresh
  strawberries
½ cup prepared Dream Whip
  topping

1. Dissolve gelatin in boiling water. Add ice cubes and stir until ice is melted. Refrigerate until mixture has thickened slightly (about 30 minutes).
2. Using a whisk, blend yogurt into gelatin mixture. Stir in ½ cup of the strawberries. Pour an equal amount of the mixture into each of four individual serving bowls. Refrigerate until mixture is firm (about 1 hour).
3. Just before serving, spoon 2 tablespoons whipped topping onto each dessert serving. Place an equal amount of remaining strawberries on each serving.

Serves 4
Approximately 1.6 grams fat per serving

COCONUT MERINGUES WITH PINEAPPLE FILLING

A lightly almond-flavored puff, edged in toasted coconut and filled with a tropical pineapple sauce.

1" × 1" piece coconut (from
    frozen packed flakes)
1 medium-sized egg white at room
    temperature
⅛ teaspoon cream of tartar
Dash salt
⅛ teaspoon vanilla extract
⅛ teaspoon almond extract
2 tablespoons sugar
⅓ cup undrained canned crushed
    pineapple in its own juice
½ teaspoon cornstarch
½ teaspoon powdered sugar
¼ teaspoon grated lemon zest

1. Preheat the broiler.
2. Crumble coconut into flakes. Broil, 2–3 inches from heat source, for about 1 minute until coconut is nicely browned (be careful not to burn it). Set aside, and reset oven to 275°F.
3. In a mixing bowl, beat egg white until foamy. Add cream of tartar, salt, and vanilla and almond extracts and beat until soft peaks form. Add sugar, one tablespoon at a time, and beat until stiff peaks form.
4. Line a baking sheet with aluminum foil. Place four uniformly sized mounds of egg white mixture onto the sheet. Smooth each mound out into a 4-inch circle and, using the back of a spoon, press down on the middle of each mound to form a well. Sprinkle toasted coconut around the outer edges of meringues. Bake for 1 hour, and then turn oven off. Leave meringues in the oven, with the door closed, for 2 hours more. Remove from oven when meringues are dry to finish cooling.
5. To prepare filling for meringues, mix together pineapple, cornstarch, powdered sugar, and lemon zest. Bring to a boil, reduce heat to simmer, and cook for 1 minute more. Remove from heat and allow mixture to cool.
6. Just before serving, spoon one-quarter of the filling into the well of each meringue.

Serves 4
Approximately 1.3 grams fat per serving

BAKED PINEAPPLE AND BANANAS

A rich, warm, "comfort food" dessert. This resembles Bananas Foster, a decadently delicious (but calorie-packed) treat.

1⅓ cups chopped fresh pineapple
⅔ cup thinly sliced ripe banana
1 tablespoon plus 1 teaspoon dark
    brown sugar (not packed)
½ teaspoon ground cinnamon
Dash ground nutmeg
Low-calorie cooking spray

1. Preheat the broiler.
2. Mix together all ingredients except cooking spray. Lightly coat a baking dish with low-calorie cooking spray and place mixture in dish. Broil, 5 inches from heat source, until bubbly (about 3 minutes). Spoon an even amount into four individual dessert dishes and serve immediately.

Serves 4
Approximately 0.1 gram fat per serving

CHOCOLATE-DRIZZLED FRUIT KABOBS

This is a marvelous dessert—fresh bananas, pineapple, and strawberries skewered and topped with a rich chocolate sauce—to top off a grilled evening meal.

½ cup ¼-inch-thick banana slices
½ cup bite-sized fresh pineapple
    pieces
½ cup halved fresh strawberries
1 tablespoon plus 2 teaspoons
    powdered sugar
1¼ teaspoons unsweetened cocoa
    powder
1½ teaspoons skim milk
⅛ teaspoon vanilla extract

1. On four individual bamboo skewers, thread equal amounts of banana slices, pineapple chunks, and strawberry halves, alternating fruit. Chill.
2. Thoroughly blend powdered sugar, cocoa, skim milk, and vanilla. Let stand for 10 minutes.
3. Just before serving, drizzle 1 teaspoon chocolate sauce over each fruit skewer. Serve immediately.

Serves 4
Approximately 0.2 gram fat per serving

CHOCOLATE DREAMS

Similar to a frozen mousse, this is a light, delicious "French Cream."

1 1.3-ounce package Dream Whip
  topping
⅓ cup skim milk
2 tablespoons water
2 tablespoons plus 1½ teaspoons
  unsweetened cocoa powder
2 medium-sized egg whites at
  room temperature
1⅓ teaspoons (4 packets) Equal
½ teaspoon vanilla extract

1. In a small bowl, combine Dream Whip, skim milk, water, and cocoa. Beat until stiff peaks form and set aside.

2. In a separate bowl, combine egg whites, Equal, and vanilla. Beat until stiff peaks form.

3. Gently but thoroughly fold egg white mixture into whipped topping mixture. Spoon an equal amount of dessert into four individual dishes. Freeze for at least 1 hour for a frozen treat, or refrigerate for 45 minutes for a more mousse-like consistency.

Serves 4
Approximately 0.1 gram fat per serving

BLUEBERRY AND LIME SORBET

Fresh blueberries blended with grape juice and fresh lime, frozen, and served in goblets.

1⅓ cups fresh blueberries
⅔ cup unsweetened grape juice
⅓ teaspoon (1 packet) Equal
1 teaspoon fresh lime juice
1 medium-sized egg white at room
  temperature
Garnish: Lime slices

1. In a food processor fitted with the steel blade or a blender, combine blueberries, grape juice, Equal, and lime juice. Blend until smooth and set aside.

2. In a separate bowl, beat egg white until stiff peaks form. Gently but thoroughly fold egg white into blueberry mixture.

3. Pour mixture into a 9-inch square glass pan. Cover with plastic wrap and place in freezer. Stir mixture once each hour. Remove from freezer when mixture has frozen (about 2 to 3 hours).

4. Place equal amounts of mixture in four individual wine goblets. Garnish each with a slice of fresh lime and serve.

Serves 4
Approximately 0.3 gram fat per serving

AMBROSIA

A sweet blend of citrus and coconut. The fruit achieves a delicious blending of flavors when refrigerated for 8 hours. It's well worth the wait.

1 medium-sized pink grapefruit
½ cup peeled navel orange sections
½ cup finely chopped fresh pineapple
3 tablespoons flaked coconut
⅓ teaspoon (1 packet) Equal, if desired

1. Preheat the broiler. Broil coconut, 2–3 inches from heat source, for about 1 minute or until coconut is nicely browned (be careful not to burn it).
2. Peel grapefruit and divide into sections. Toss all ingredients together and refrigerate for at least 8 hours.
3. Place an equal amount of mixture into four individual chilled serving dishes.

Serves 4
Approximately 1.4 grams fat per serving

FIVE-FRUIT CUP

A heavenly combination of fresh fruits tossed in a rich, sweet cream.

½ medium-sized apple
½ medium-sized navel orange, peeled and sectioned
½ cup bite-sized fresh pineapple pieces
¾ cup bite-sized fresh peach pieces
½ cup halved seedless green grapes
½ cup nonfat plain yogurt
½ teaspoon vanilla extract
⅛ teaspoon cinnamon
⅓ teaspoon (1 packet) Equal

1. In a glass bowl, mix together all of the fruits. Chill for at least 2 hours.
2. Mix together yogurt, vanilla extract, cinnamon, and Equal. Chill until ready to serve dessert.
3. Just before serving, place an equal amount of fruit mixture into four individual dessert dishes and top each with 2 tablespoons yogurt.

Serves 5
Approximately 0.4 gram fat per serving

CHOCOLATE CRUMB "CREME DE MENTHE"

A minty cream dessert topped with a layer of chocolate cookie crumbs.

1½ teaspoons sugar-free lime
  gelatin
½ cup boiling water
½ teaspoon vanilla extract
¼ teaspoon peppermint extract
⅛ teaspoon brandy extract, if
  desired
5 ice cubes
1 cup prepared Dream Whip
  topping
5 chocolate wafers, ground coarse

1. Mix together gelatin, water, and extracts. Stir until gelatin has dissolved. Add ice cubes and stir until ice has melted.

2. Gently fold whipped topping into gelatin mixture until well blended. Pour an equal amount (about ½ cup) into each of four dessert bowls. Chill for 1 hour.

3. Just before serving, sprinkle an equal amount of chocolate crumbs over each serving.

Serves 4
Approximately 1.6 grams fat per serving

PINEAPPLE SUPREME

Sweet lemon and pineapple cream capped with crunchy graham cracker crumbs.

½ cup drained canned crushed
  pineapple in its own juice, juice
  reserved
Additional unsweetened pineapple
  juice if needed to make ¼ cup
1½ teaspoons sugar-free lemon
  gelatin
⅓ cup evaporated skim milk, well
  chilled
½ teaspoon vanilla extract
2 2½" × 2½" graham crackers,
  ground coarse

1. In a small pot, bring ¼ cup juice to a boil. Add gelatin and stir until dissolved. Mix in pineapple. Place mixture in freezer.

2. Place evaporated skim milk and vanilla extract in a small bowl. Whip until mixture has the consistency of whipped cream.

3. Remove gelatin mixture from freezer. Gently but thoroughly fold whipped milk mixture into gelatin. Place an equal amount of dessert into each of four serving bowls. Chill for 5 to 6 hours.

4. Just before serving, sprinkle an equal amount of graham cracker crumbs over each dessert serving.

Serves 4
Approximately 0.9 gram fat per serving

TROPICAL CITRUS FREEZE

A truly refreshing orange, pineapple, lemon, and lime ice.

2 tablespoons sugar
⅔ teaspoon (2 packets) Equal
1¼ cups water
⅓ cup fresh orange juice
⅓ cup unsweetened pineapple
    juice
2 tablespoons fresh lemon juice
2 tablespoons fresh lime juice
1 teaspoon grated orange zest

1. Mix together sugar, Equal, and water until sugar is thoroughly dissolved. Add remaining ingredients and mix well.

2. Pour mixture into a 9-inch square pan. Place in the freezer and chill for 2 to 3 hours, stirring once every hour until mixture is the consistency of a slush.

3. Spoon dessert into four individual bowls and serve.

Serves 4
Approximately 0.2 gram fat per serving

BANANA CREAM SUPREME

A delicate blend of fresh bananas, creamy pudding, and nutmeg.

3 tablespoons sugar-free
    vanilla-flavored instant pudding
    mix
1 cup skim milk
¼ cup water
½ small very ripe banana, mashed
1 medium-sized egg white at room
    temperature
½ teaspoon vanilla extract
Ground nutmeg to taste

1. In a mixing bowl, combine pudding mix, skim milk, and water. Stir for 1 minute. Blend in mashed banana and set aside.

2. In a small bowl, beat egg white and vanilla together until stiff peaks form.

3. Gently but thoroughly fold egg·white mixture into pudding. Spoon an equal amount (about ½ cup) into each of four dessert bowls. Sprinkle each with nutmeg. Serve immediately or cover and refrigerate until serving time.

Serves 4
Approximately 0.1 gram fat per serving

STRAWBERRY-CROWNED LEMON CHIFFON

Creamy lemon squares layered with graham cracker crumbs, whipped topping, and ripe fresh strawberries.

1½ teaspoons sugar-free lemon
  gelatin
¾ cup boiling water
2 ice cubes
½ cup vanilla-flavored low-fat
  yogurt
¼ teaspoon grated lemon zest
⅓ cup thinly sliced fresh
  strawberries
⅙ teaspoon (½ packet) Equal
2 2½″ × 2½″ graham crackers,
  grated coarse
2 tablespoons plus 2 teaspoons
  prepared Dream Whip topping

1. In a mixing bowl, dissolve gelatin in boiling water. Add ice cubes and stir until ice has melted. Add yogurt and lemon zest and beat until thoroughly blended. Place mixture in the freezer and chill for 20 minutes.

2. Remove mixture from freezer. Using an electric mixer, whip until fluffy (about 3 minutes). Spoon into a loaf pan. Refrigerate for 3 hours.

3. In a small bowl, mix together strawberries and Equal. Refrigerate until serving time.

4. Just before serving, sprinkle graham cracker crumbs evenly over gelatin mixture. Slice into four squares, and place each square on a dessert dish. Top each serving with an equal amount (about 2 teaspoons) of whipped topping and an equal amount (about 1½ tablespoons) of strawberries.

Serves 4
Approximately 1 gram fat per serving

MERINGUES WITH CHOCOLATE MOUSSE

Fragile, airy puffs filled with a delicious chocolate cream.

Meringues:
1 medium-sized egg white at room
  temperature
1/8 teaspoon cream of tartar
1/8 teaspoon salt
1/4 teaspoon vanilla extract
1/4 teaspoon almond extract
1/3 cup sugar

Chocolate Mousse:
1/2 cup skim milk
1 tablespoon plus 1 teaspoon
  sugar-free chocolate-flavored
  instant pudding mix
1/2 cup prepared Dream Whip
  topping

1. Preheat oven to 275°F.

2. Using an electric mixer, beat egg white until foamy. Add cream of tartar, salt, and vanilla and almond extracts. Beat until soft peaks form. Add sugar, 1 tablespoon at a time, and beat until stiff peaks form.

3. Line a baking sheet with aluminum foil. Spoon an equal amount of mixture in four mounds onto the sheet. Smooth each mound into a 4-inch circle and, using a spoon, press into the center of each to form a well.

4. Bake for 1 hour. Turn oven off and leave meringues in the oven, with the door closed, for 2 hours more. Remove meringues from oven to finish cooling.

5. In a bowl, combine skim milk with pudding mix. Stir well and let stand for 5 minutes.

6. Gently but thoroughly fold whipped topping into pudding.

7. Just before serving, spoon 2½ tablespoons pudding mixture into the well of each meringue. Serve immediately.

Serves 4
Approximately 0.4 gram fat per serving

PLAIN AND SIMPLE 50-CALORIE DESSERTS

Quick, easy-to-make desserts for when you don't have time to prepare a more elaborate treat. With these fix-in-a-hurry ideas, there is always time for dessert.

Apples: ⅔ cup sliced equals one 50-calorie serving. For a bit of extra flavor, sprinkle ground cinnamon over the slices. Approximately 0.3 gram fat per serving.

Applesauce: ⅔ cup unsweetened equals one 50-calorie serving. Ground cinnamon makes a nice garnish. Approximately 0.3 gram fat per serving.

Apricots: 2 small fresh *or* 3 medium-sized halves canned (packed in their own juice) equal one 50-calorie serving. Approximately 0.2 gram fat per serving.

Blueberries: ½ cup fresh equals one 50-calorie serving. Approximately 0.4 gram fat per serving.

Butter Mints: 7 mints equal one 50-calorie serving. Approximately 0.3 gram fat per serving.

Cantaloupe: ⅔ cup cubed equals one 50-calorie serving. Approximately 0.1 gram fat per serving.

Cherries (Dark Sweet): 10 large fresh equal one 50-calorie serving. Approximately 0.2 gram fat per serving.

Chocolate Kisses (Bite-Sized): 2 equal one 50-calorie serving. Approximately 3 grams fat per serving.

Gelatin with Whipped Topping: 2 cups sugar-free gelatin with 2 tablespoons prepared Dream Whip topping equal one 50-calorie serving. Approximately 0.8 gram fat per serving.

Graham Crackers: One 2½″ × 6″ cracker equals one 50-calorie serving. Approximately 1.3 grams fat per serving.

Grapes (Red or Green): ⅓ cup fresh equals one 50-calorie serving. Approximately 0.1 gram fat per serving.

Gum Drops (Bite-Sized): 14 equal one 50-calorie serving. Approximately 0.1 gram fat per serving.

Honeydew: ⅔ cup cubed equals one 50-calorie serving. Approximately 0.4 gram fat per serving.

Jelly Beans (Small): 8 equal one 50-calorie serving. Approximately 0.1 gram fat per serving.

Malted Milk Balls (Small, Chocolate-coated): 5 equal one 50-calorie serving. Approximately 2.5 grams fat per serving.

Nectarines: 1½ medium-sized equal one 50-calorie serving. Approximately 0.1 gram fat per serving.

Oranges: ½ cup fresh sections equals one 50-calorie serving. Approximately 0.2 gram fat per serving.

Peaches: ¾ cup fresh slices equals one 50-calorie serving. Approximately 0.1 gram fat per serving.

Pears: ⅔ cup fresh slices equals one 50-calorie serving. Approximately 0.2 gram fat per serving.

Pepperidge Farm "Bordeaux" Cookies: 2 equal one 50-calorie serving. Approximately 3.5 grams fat per serving.

Pineapple: ¾ cup fresh cubes *or* 1 slice canned in its own juice equals one 50-calorie serving. Approximately 0.2 gram fat per serving.

Raspberries (Red):   ⅔ cup fresh equals one 50-calorie serving. Approximately 1.4 grams fat per serving.

Strawberries: 1 cup sliced fresh equals one 50-calorie serving. Approximately 0.8 gram fat per serving.

Tangerines: 2 small equal one 50-calorie serving. Approximately 0.2 gram fat per serving.

Vanilla Wafers: 3 equal one 50-calorie serving. Approximately 1.8 grams fat per serving.

Watermelon: 1 cup cubed equals one 50-calorie serving. Approximately 0.2 gram fat per serving.

❖ INDEX ❖